THE BEST OF

G. Campbell Morgan

THE BEST OF

G. Campbell Morgan

Edited by
Ralph Turnbull

BAKER BOOK HOUSE
Grand Rapids, Michigan

Contents

Introduction 7

Christ and the Bible 15
    from *The Westminster Booklets*

Paul's Estimate of Life 34
    from *The True Estimate of Life*

The Hidden Years 50
    from *The Hidden Years at Nazareth*

But One Thing 62
    from *The Westminster Booklets*

Foundations 77
    from *The Westminster Booklets*

To Die Is Gain 90
    from *The Westminster Booklets*

The Spirit of the Age 109
    from *Wherein?*

The Purifying Hope 117
    from *God's Methods with Man*

The Church Evangelistic 127
    from *Evangelism*

The Unity of the Church 140
    from *The Westminster Record*

The Dominion of Man 154
    from *The Westminster Bible Record*

This Darkness 167
    from *God, Humanity and the War*

Disciples for Building and Battling 179
    from *A Series of Sermons*

The Mediating Ministry of the Holy Spirit 190
    from *Categorical Imperatives of the Christian Faith*

The Finality of the Speech of God through the Son 201
    from *The Westminster Record*

A Man Whose Name Was Job 209
    from *The Answers of Jesus to Job*

Yea, Hath God Said? 219
    from *The Voice of the Devil*

Bibliography 226

INTRODUCTION

In estimating the value and worth of his preaching and teaching, we are always thrown back to the Bible itself. George Campbell Morgan (1863-1945) did not attempt to speak of himself, but in all humility of spirit gave witness to the Word of God as the foundation and substance for all that he would say. He was essentially an Interpreter. No matter what he did in public speech he referred to the Word of God. Thus if one would begin to place him in the history of preaching or in the work of the Church he is seen as a Bible Expositor. Even the small devotional pamphlets or the occasional lectures or talks, apart from regular sermon series, show evidence of his careful research from the Bible.

The clue to his mentality and method lies in what he said in Lectures on Preaching, given at Cheshunt College, Cambridge, and at the Biblical Seminary, New York. In the volume entitled *Preaching,* he states in "The Essentials of a Sermon" that he never heard a lecture on Homiletics in his life, yet he had given a good many. He said, "I have tried to examine in the New Testament, and in the Old Testament, the great preaching of both the prophets of the Old and the apostles and evangelists of the New. And if I am asked to condense into words the essentials of a sermon, I do it with these three: *Truth, Clarity, Passion.*"

In a nutshell, there is Morgan at his best — and always the same. Whether we sample his early writings in sermon form or in an occasional devotional talk or in a formal lecture about the

Bible, the same is apparent. He was a man of one book! Thus every message was the outcome of the study of the whole. Truth, Clarity, Passion — were the characteristics of Morgan's preaching-teaching.

The question might be asked: What progression is there in his teaching? What difference is there in the mature Morgan from the beginner in the ministry? And, did he change his mind about essential doctrines? These are important questions and a partial answer may be attempted in the light of a survey of his works and writings.

In *This Was His Faith*, The Expository Letters of G. Campbell Morgan, compiled and edited by Jill Morgan, reference is made to "Controversy Over Details Unprofitable" with regard to the so-called "Rapture" at the Second Coming. He definitely changed his views on this. In *God's Methods With Man* he espoused the pre-millennial interpretation and this he reaffirmed to the end. However, within that context he gave up belief in "the Rapture" and also the idea of "a missing week in Daniel." His general views of the fact of the Second Advent were unchanged throughout his ministry, except that in these particulars he came to concur with the views of Philip Mauro. He also regretted the controversy which had divided God's people on this crucial doctrine. Perhaps that made him pause in days of maturity from expounding the details which once aroused his interest. The fact of Christ's Return was never in doubt. (The writer has in his possession a personal letter from Dr. Morgan explaining these changes of belief and in his preaching-teaching ministry.)

John Harries in *G. Campbell Morgan*, the Man and His Ministry, has said: "Insight, imagination, large discernment, human sympathy and broad, charitable understanding, combine with certain natural gifts, clarity of expression, lucidity of definition and the like, to make of Dr. Morgan a Biblical expositor almost without a peer. In his hands, the Bible — its pages, precepts, character – is made positively to live and to exude an enheartening, a vital force."

In this Treasury no attempt is made to select items from the long list of books which comprise his major expository works. The list of his books will be given at the close. The list indicates the widespread nature of Morgan's interest and the attempt to bring the whole Bible under tribute to the end of teaching and preaching. This Treasury does not include selections from *The Westminster Pulpit; Searchlights from the Word; The Messages of the Bible; The Analyzed Bible;* his sermonic expositions of *The Four Gospels, The Acts of the Apostles, The Corinthian Letters* of Paul, *The Prophecy of Jeremiah,* as well as many others on books and subjects of Biblical interest. As most of these are kept in print it is not necessary to duplicate. This selection is based upon rarer items and occasional addresses so that another aspect of Morgan's ministry may be estimated.

The saga of George Campbell Morgan's life and work has its inception when he was a young school teacher who found openings to conduct services on Sundays. His early promise led to the examination and trial for the ministry of the Methodist Church. By an unusual providence the judges then rejected him at the "trial sermon" he delivered before a few people. Later, he was to be the guest preacher to the Methodist Conference at the height of his public eminence as a preacher. On that occasion he could remind his Methodist friends that he had been "turned down" by them. However, there was no rancor – only a humble endeavor to find the will of God for his life. In this he was led to the Congregational Church and its open door by the local congregation. The rest that followed is the romance of preaching. From one small church to another he made his way in a short time until finally he was called to Westminster Chapel, London. Here he gave the best years of his life, and then after travel and ministries in America he returned for a final spell in that well-known pulpit. All this is spelled out in *A Man of The Word,* by

Jill Morgan; *Campbell Morgan Bible Teacher,* by Harold Murray, as well as other contributions about his work in symposia and books dealing with outstanding preachers.

In stature Morgan was tall and imposing with his white hair and leonine cast of feature. Savonarola's face is not unlike the modern Morgan who also preached to crowds of people and of whom it could be said he was God's prophet and voice to the city. His preaching to congregations regularly twice on a Sunday was matched by his Friday weeknight Bible Lecture. When not on travel to distant parts for a wider ministry, Morgan for most of his ministry gave expositions of books of the Bible on Fridays. 1,500 to 2,000 people gathered in those years of 1904-1914. He returned in 1933-1943, and only retired at the age of eighty. At the end of 1929 he had travelled over 714,000 miles, crossed the Atlantic 49 times, and preached 20,000 sermons. By any test he was phenomenal. His secret? If any, it lay in his daily concentration on Bible study. Nothing – not even travel or wider ministries – interfered with that requirement of study. Morgan followed the days of D. L. Moody's evangelistic campaigns, both in Great Britain and in America. Possibly this was a contributing factor to his success. After the evangelist, the church and the public then needed the teacher and interpreter.

To have heard Morgan at his height was an unforgettable experience – the large congregation; the expectancy; the initial worship; then the climactic exposition of a part of the Bible. Morgan was at his best in dealing with a passage of Scripture. He had read and reread it; then exegeted it; now he expounded its meaning, but always seeing it in the context of the whole book or the whole Bible. His rich, bell-tone voice was used to advantage as he played this organ for a large congregation – with the variation of mood and feeling as he moved along his customary path of exposition. Gaunt and almost ascetic in appearance, the prose and vocabulary were pure English, and the passionate utterance pleaded for conviction and response. Whether at

Westminster, London or at Northfield Conference (with D. L. Moody), Massachusetts, the response was the same — no one heard without profit to Bible teaching like this.

RALPH G. TURNBULL

THE BEST OF

G. Campbell Morgan

CHRIST AND THE BIBLE

THIS LECTURE is a statement of conviction, and a declaration of position.

We are in the midst of a remarkable period in matters theological. Voices, arresting attention, are being heard. They are expressing views which are in conflict with each other.

Sometimes, alas! the tones of personal bitterness are discernible. Let me at once affirm my desire to recognize the sincerity of all who are taking part in this discussion. From the views of some, I differ radically, but I am ready to recognize their absolute honesty of conviction, and their right to give expression to such conviction. They will as readily grant so much to those who differ from them.

Those conducting the discussions may broadly be divided into two camps, supernaturalists and naturalists, and for the present discussion that resolves itself into a division between

1. Those who believe that the Bible is the Infallible Word of God.

2. Those who do not so believe.

In each of these camps there are differences of opinion. Those believing the Bible to be the Word of God differ greatly in their interpretation of its teaching. Those who do not so believe also hold widely divergent theories. It is not my intention now to discuss the many views in either camp. Neither is it my purpose to put into contrast the two positions, save as the statement of one, will necessarily do so.

My own ministry is based upon the conviction that the Bible is the Infallible Word of God, and I desire to state my reasons for this conviction.

My position may briefly be stated thus. I believe that there is an indissoluble relation between the Christ of the catholic Christian experience, and the Bible. By the term "catholic Christian experience" I intend, not the consciousness of any one individual, nor the views held by any group of Christian people; but the spiritual and moral consciousness resulting from the actual victories won by Christianity during the past nineteen centuries. The Christ of this experience is related to the Bible as the Living Word is related to the Written. To change the conception of the first, is necessarily to change the form of the second. To change the form of the second, is to change the conception of the first.

Let me state this in another way. What we do with the Christ of the catholic church — using the word "catholic" in its proper sense — we shall do with the Bible. What we do with the Bible we must ultimately do with the Christ of the catholic church.

As to the first.

> To deny His supernatural nature, is necessarily to deny the authenticity of the Bible story.
>
> To deny His infallibility, is to deny that of the Bible.
>
> To deny His atonement as interpreted in the New Testament, is to account the whole Hebrew idea of approach to God by sacrifice as barbaric.

As to the second.

> To deny the history of the Bible, is to be without any history of Jesus.
>
> To deny the possibility of the miracles they affirm, is to deny the stories of His Virgin birth and bodily resurrection.

To deny their records of His teaching, is no longer to be sure of anything He said.

Christ and the Bible then, are interdependent for existence. That, broadly stated, is my theme. In discussing it I shall ask you to consider with me

Christ and the New Testament.
Christ and the Old Testament.

I
HIS RELATION TO THE NEW TESTAMENT

First, then, His relation to the New Testament. Regarding this I make these statements.

1. The New Testament is the Book of the Christ.
2. The Christian religion is the religion of the Christ of the New Testament.
3. The propagation of Christianity has always depended upon the testimony of eye-witnesses, as recorded in the Scriptures of the New Testament.

1. *The New Testament is the Book of the Christ.* I do not suppose that anyone will challenge the validity of that statement. For the moment the question of the accuracy of the records is not before us, but only that of their uniqueness as claiming to give any detailed account of the Founder of the Christian Faith. If these stories be denied, what have we left? A Person in history certainly, for references are made to Him in other writings which establish His historical actuality, but they give us no definite information regarding His parentage, or life, or character. Profane history has done no more than recognize His actual existence. Take away the New Testament, and there yet remains the certainty of the Person called Jesus, but no positive or detailed information concerning Him.

It is a simple but fundamental fact that the New Testament is the only literature concerning Jesus Christ. There is, of course, a marvellous literature, ever growing, and richer growing, with the passing years, which is based upon the accuracy of the New Testament records. That, however, is wholly valueless if the New Testament itself is destroyed.

Let us impress this first fact upon our minds by passing the New Testament in rapid survey.

In the first four books we have a presentation of the Person of Jesus.

In the Acts of the Apostles we have the story of the early triumphs of those who believed the stories of Jesus which the Gospel narratives record.

In the Epistles we have a body of writing in which the teaching of Jesus is elaborated and expounded.

In the Book of Revelation we have, as its title indicates, the Unveiling of the same Person.

Thus throughout the subject is Christ;

His Person in the Gospels.

His Power in the Acts.

His Precepts in the Epistles.

His Program in the Revelation.

Take the Gospel stories first, not discussing for the moment their authenticity. They present to us a Person who can only thus be described;

God, incarnate.

Man, unfallen, unsinning, absolutely fulfilling the highest ideal of manhood.

The Saviour of the unfit by the way of the Cross, and by no other way.

The Lord, not primarily by His teaching, nor by His example, but by the infinite, final miracle of His resurrection from among the dead.

Whether these things are true or not, I repeat, is not for the moment the question with which I am dealing. I simply assert that these can only be denied by denying the truth of the records. These facts constitute the Harmony of the four stories.

Each writer has presented to us, moreover, a different aspect of the office or nature of the Person. As to office, Matthew describes Him as King, and we see Him in His royalty; while Mark presents Him to us as a Servant, absolutely surrendered to the will of God. As to nature, Luke, with the genius of the true artist, portrays Him in the matchless perfection of His human nature; while John enabling us to touch more familiarly than any other the warm flesh of the Man of Nazareth, yet causes us to feel the thrill of Deity.

The fourfold Gospel thus presents this Person. I study it, and I see a King who serves, a Servant who reigns; a Man fulfilling absolutely the highest ideal of life, and yet One who transcends all these descriptions, until the fisher of the Galilean lake who leaned his head upon His bosom, and listened to the beating of His heart, describes Him in the mystic words, "The Word became flesh, and dwelt among us, and we beheld His glory." Such is the Person that the Gospel presents; and if He be no real Being, then so perfectly does the picture command my loyalty, and my worship, that I say, In God's name lead me to the man who imagined Him.

I turn to the book of the Acts of the Apostles. It is well to remember that the titles of the books of the Bible are not inspired. This title is certainly most unfortunate. Some of the apostles are never mentioned after their names are included in the list at the first, and of the acts of those mentioned a very few are recorded. A title far more accurate would be, *The Continuation of the Doing and Teaching of the Christ by the Holy Spirit through the Members of His Mystical Body, the Church.* Luke commences this second treatise to his friend Theophilus, "The former treatise I made, O Theophilus, concerning all that Jesus *began* to do and to teach." By that commencement he at least suggests that he is about to continue the story, and as the book is read this proves indeed to be a key to its interpretation. The Person presented in the Gospels, is seen again on every page of this second treatise. The kingly Christ is reincarnate in kingly men, who conquer as they go. The serving Christ is reproduced in a multitude of serving souls. The ideal Man is found in multitudes who manifest a type of life such as the world had never seen. The manifestation of God is continued in those who, being "partakers of the Divine nature," show forth the excellencies of Him who called them out of darkness into light.

This, then, is still the story of the Christ, no longer limited and localized, or, to use His own word as recorded by Luke, "straitened," as He was in the days of His sojourn among men, but proceeding in spiritual power through the ever increasing number of His saints to do the work of God and teach His will to men.

I turn to the Epistles. We are told today that it is necessary to go back from Paul to Christ. I declare that this is impossible, because Paul never departed by a hair's breadth from Christ. In the Pauline statement of truth concerning Christ there is nothing out of harmony with the presentation of His Person in the Gospels and the revelation of His power in the Acts. It is perfectly true that there are some things in the writings of Paul which had local reference, but these also reveal principles. Everything of systematic teaching found in the Pauline writings may be traced to the teaching of Jesus. The recorded words of Jesus were always simple, but never with the simplicity of superficiality. So profound were they that exposition has never been able to exhaust them. I believe that there is yet much more light and truth to break forth from His words. That is to me an argument for the lonely splendor of His Personality; and so is the fact that in the Epistles we have unfoldings of His meaning, and that rightly interpreted they are in perfect harmony with His teaching, revealing at once the sublimity of His words, and the value of these writings. I affirm that all the writings of Paul and Peter, of James and John, and that of Jude, are but expositions of the teaching of Jesus by the inspiration of the Holy Spirit, according to His promise made in the Paschal discourses. The proof of this must be sought in a study of these writings in the light of the things He said.

Let me take one illustration. I am told that the Church is a Pauline conception. There is an element of truth in that statement, for it is certain that he himself considered that he was specially a steward of the mystery of the Church. But in the two or three brief sentences which Christ uttered concerning His Church there is the germ of all the system which Paul taught. The words of Jesus at Caesarea Philippi were full of suggestiveness. The great movement of His propaganda was at an end. Gathering His disciples about Him, He inquired, "Who do men say that the Son of man is?" We are familiar with the answers they gave, and with the fact that they did not satisfy Him. He made His appeal directly to them: "But who say ye that I am?" Peter's answer was complete: "Thou art the Christ, the Son of the living God." Then immediately He spoke of His Church: "I also say unto thee, that thou art Peter, and upon this rock I will build my church; and the gates of Hades shall not prevail against it."

Notice carefully that in this statement there is a two-fold declaration. First, "I will build my church." In the Corinthian and Ephesian letters Paul has described this Church, showing how it "groweth into a holy temple in the Lord." But Christ had said everything when He declared "I will build my church." Second, "the gates of Hades shall not prevail against it." This does not mean, I will build it so strongly that the gates of Hades cannot overthrow it. That would be a false figure, for an attacking city does not carry its gates with it. In the first declaration He has said that His Church will be impregnable. What He builds upon rock foundation no force can overthrow. In the second He reveals the fact that the Church is to be an aggressive force; and with the farsightedness of the Master Campaigner, He surveys the whole field of conflict, and referring to the last enemy, declares, "the gates of Hades shall not prevail against it."

Paul subsequently described the conflict of the Church, declaring, "Our wrestling is not against flesh and blood, but against the principalities, against the powers, against the world-rulers of this darkness, against the spiritual hosts of wickedness in the heavenly places," and he charged us "to stand ... withstand ... to stand." But all this was included in the Master's vision, and the final standing was indicated in the declaration that the "gates of Hades shall not prevail against it."

This is but an illustration of the fact that all the essential truths elaborated in the Epistles are to be found in unified form in the words of Jesus which have been recorded for us in the Gospel narratives.

Turning finally to the Apocalypse. Its opening phrase is a revelation of its supreme value; "The Unveiling of Jesus Christ." Amid all the mysterious imagery of living ones, and vials and trumpets and seals, One Person is manifest. It is He to whom we were introduced in the Gospels, whose spiritual power was revealed in the Acts, and whose teaching has been unfolded in the Epistles. Here He is seen in a majesty and glory which are full of beauty, "girt about at the breasts with a golden girdle," with many diadems upon His brow, affirming, "I am Alpha and Omega," announcing, "I make all things new," and assuring His waiting ones, "I come quickly."

2. Again, *the Christian religion is the religion of the Christ of the New Testament*. Through nineteen centuries the Christian religion has steadily and surely grown. Through many vicissitudes, and like the incoming tide, by ebb and flow, it has advanced in spite of all outside opposition, and often in spite of internal failure. This advance has, until now, been the advance of the religion of the Christ which the New Testament pre-

sents. If by the use of the past tense in that statement I seem to presuppose the possibility of some new interpretation of the Christ superseding the old, I can only say that I have no such hope — or fear.

If for any reason there are those who think it necessary or right to attempt an interpretation of Jesus which denies the accuracy of the New Testament records, we can only say that before any such interpretation can be seriously considered it must win its victories. These must be at least equal to those already won. When it has, not in isolated instances merely, but in successive centuries, turned sinners into saints, righted social wrongs, transformed national character, freed slaves, lifted womanhood, cared for children, built hospitals, then, and not till then, will it have demonstrated its right to be put into comparison with the religion of the Christ of the New Testament. And even then it must begin where Christianity began, with pagan or savage people. It cannot be permitted to start on the foundation already laid by the Christian faith as it has been understood until now.

All these victories have been won by that religion which is based upon the New Testament interpretation of the Christ, which declares that He was God incarnate, perfect Man, Saviour by the way of the Cross, and Lord by the resurrection. This is a declaration which defies denial. In every age, among all people, this presentation of Christ has been victorious in changing unfit men into such as have blessed their age and constituted the true strength of social and national life.

It may be necessary — I know not, and I am not careful to know — to find some new religion for intellectual souls who have never sinned — if such there be. This one thing is certain, that during these centuries no other interpretation of Christ has ever attracted men for long, or saved them when it has attracted them; and in a world so full or sorrow and sighing and sin, the only religion which is of any real value is that which begins with the lowest, and is able to transform into the highest.

3. Finally, *the propagation of Christianity has always depended upon the testimony of eye-witnesses, which testimony is recorded for us in the Scriptures of the New Testament.*

Referring again to the writing of Luke, the one evangelist who was not an eye-witness, it is interesting to notice how carefully he insists that his story is constructed of material supplied by eye-witnesses. At the first, those who had seen and heard the doing and teaching of Jesus recounted the stories. Then some of their number committed these stories to writing. It is granted now that the Gospel narratives as we have them were written earlier than some critics of a generation ago imagined. Sir William Ramsay has shown that the theory which obtained in certain schools for a long time, that the Gospel stories were to be placed among the Antonines, is untenable. He says, "No person, who is capable of appreciating the tone and thought of different periods, could place the composition of any of the books of the New Testament in the period of the Antonines, unless he were imperfectly informed of the character and spirit of that period; and the fact that some modern scholars have placed them (or some of them) in that period merely shows with what light-hearted haste some scholars have proceeded to decide on difficult subjects without acquisition of the knowledge imperatively required, before a fair judgment could be pronounced. . . . The idea and narrative of the birth of Christ could not be a growth of mythology at a later time, even during the period A.D. 60-100, but sprang from the conditions and thoughts, and expressed itself in the words of the period to which it professes to belong." There can thus be no doubt that some of these stories were written by the very men who saw the things described. These written records of eye-witnesses became the accepted chronicles of facts concerning the Christ, and subsequent preaching and teaching of the Christian faith depended upon their accuracy.

Thus, through every century, either by speech or in writings, the story of eye-witnesses has been the means by which the victories of the Church have been won. Whenever in the process of history these writings have been lost, or hidden from men, the moral effect which their preaching produces has been lost also. We speak of the dark ages. What was the reason of the darkness? The withdrawal from the people of those writings in which the story of the eye-witnesses is to be found. The central fact of the Reformation — the blessed and glorious Reformation — was the restoration of the people of these stories of the eye-witnesses, the records of the Christ. With their restoration the lost moral values were restored. To this contention it has been objected that in those dark ages there lived some of the finest saints that Christianity ever produced. But it must not be forgotten that they were such as lived in the monastic establishments where they had access to the Writings, as their own writings testify. If today, by any process, we lose these Writings, we shall certainly lose the moral values which have been created by them. So surely as the people are robbed of the Scriptures — whether by a new priestism of scholarship which declares the plain man cannot read his Bible, or by denying their truth — they will be robbed of the moral force which has made and uplifted them.

These moral victories demonstrate the accuracy of the New Testament records. If the records be destroyed, the victories cannot. History cannot be unwritten. Then, if indeed the records are either a fiction or a fraud, or both, we are face to face with an impossible situation. The greatest force which the world has ever known for individual salvation, for social renewal, for national ennoblement, has been generated by the perpetual proclamation of statements which are untrue. Truth has flourished by the persistent repetition of a lie. Righteousness has triumphed by belief in a fraud. That would be a greater miracle than any the Bible records. The supposition is impossible. The nature of

Christian triumphs is such as to set a seal upon the New Testament which cannot be broken.

II
HIS RELATION TO THE OLD TESTAMENT

We may now turn to a consideration of the relation of Christ to the Old Testament. It is necessary, however, to state that this second half of our consideration is directly dependent upon what already has been advanced. If the historic accuracy and consequent authority of the New Testament be denied, nothing I now say will be conclusive. If, on the other hand, they are accepted, we may make our appeal to the New Testament concerning the relation which Christ bears to the Old.

This consideration I propose to divide into two parts:

1. Christ's testimony before His Cross.
2. Christ's testimony after His Resurrection.

1. *Christ's testimony before His Cross.* The whole life of Jesus was conditioned by the law of the Old Testament Scriptures. The ceremonies connected with His birth — His confirmation as a boy of twelve, His relation to the Sabbath day, His use of the Jewish feasts — all prove that His life was by training, and ultimately by choice, amenable to that law. From His first recorded word through all His subsequent doing and teaching it is evident that He recognized the Divine authority of the Mosaic economy. Under stress of temptation He rebutted the attacks of the foe by standing squarely within the law as given by Moses. His every quotation in answer to the suggestions of the devil was taken therefrom.

During the period of His public ministry He never called in question by a single word the authority of the Old Testament. More than once He corrected prevalent misinterpretations of its meaning, but His teaching was constantly based upon its declarations. Indeed, it is in accordance with the strictest accuracy to say that He said nothing which had not already been written in the Scriptures of the Hebrew people. All He taught was new, but its freshness was that of interpretation of truth, and its redemption from the wrong which had been done to it by those who had never rightly understood it. His actual quotations from, and allusions to the Old Testament were constant. Out of the thirty-nine books, He quoted in the course of His ministry from twenty-four, in words actually recorded for us. Approximately, there are to be found sixty-six quotations from, or allusions to the Pentateuch, forty from Isaiah, thirty-six from the Psalms, and twenty-two from Daniel — yes, positively from Daniel! There is no escape from the conviction that Jesus treated the Old Testament as Divine, and therefore authoritative.

This is admitted by those who are not prepared to admit that the Old Testament ought to be looked upon as the Word of God. Their explanation of Christ's attitude is a remarkable one, and involves a conception of Christ which is in itself out of harmony with the revelation of the New Testament. They declare that He was in human life merely a child of His age. I think it is sometimes well to translate a statement like this into the rougher language of greater clearness, and therefore I affirm that this means that His attitude to the Old Testament was due to His ignorance. I do not think I am unfair when I so interpret such an attitude. Several years ago, in conversation with one holding that view, I put the following blunt question, "Do you really believe that in these matters Jesus of Nazareth knew less than — let me say for the sake of illustration — Cheyne?" Without hesitation he replied, "Yes, I certainly hold that modern scholars know more on questions of authorship than Christ could know."

Of course, from the standpoint of my Christology such a statement makes further discussion on biblical subjects impossible. That is to say, there is a prior question which must be decided — that, namely, of the Person of Christ. This statement will be granted as true by all; therefore I am compelled to turn for a moment to that subject.

This interpretation of the attitude of Christ to the Old Testament is based upon a theory of the Kenosis. It is impossible fully to discuss that theory in the course of what at most can only be a passing reference. Nevertheless it is equally impossible to entirely pass it by.

The theory is based upon an interpretation of something written by Paul. I am careful to say that it is based upon an *interpretation*. I should more accurately describe my own conviction by affirming that it is based upon a *misinterpretation*. I am careful, therefore, not to say that the theory is based on something which Paul wrote. In the Philippian letter occur these familiar and sublime words, "Who, being in the form of God, counted it not a prize to be on an equality with God, but emptied himself, taking the form of a servant, being made in the likeness of man; and being found in fashion as a man, he humbled himself, becoming obedient even unto death, yea, the death of the cross." The theory of the Konosis is based upon an interpretation of the meaning of the declaration, "he emptied himself." It declares that this means that He abandoned Deity, and became human merely. Therefore it is concluded He knew no more than the men of the age into which He came.

It is with this interpretation I join issue. I deny that Paul intends by the declaration "he emptied himself" to convey the idea that He laid aside His Deity. Throughout the whole of this passage one Person is before the mind. He is the same essentially, before the emptying, in the stupendous act thereof, and subsequently, "he emptied himself," but He did not cease to be Himself.

What, then, is the meaning of the declaration? The answer will be found in the occurrence of the word "form" before and after the declaration. "Being in the form of God," "taking the form of a servant," "he emptied himself" of one form of manifestation, in order to take another form of manifestation. I hold that in the infinite mystery of the Trinity the eternal Son is the

One through whom, and through whom alone, God is ever manifest either in heaven or on earth, to angels or to any created being. I believe that during the period in which the eternal Son was veiled in flesh, heaven lacked, not the presence, but the manifestation of Deity. The Kenosis consisted in the laying aside of the form of manifestation suited to unfallen and unsinning creation; and the taking of that form in which it was possible for fallen and sinning men to see the Father.

Thus I believe that the eternal Son was very Man in the midst of men, and yet other than man. I am quite conscious of the mystery of such a Person, but my inability to explain is not sufficient warrant for the denial of the teaching of the Scriptures, which has resulted in such victories in human history to which I have already referred.

Great as the mystery is, I believe that Jesus of Nazareth was Man, but other than man; was flesh, but also the "Word made flesh"; and that in all His life there was the consciousness of Deity.

If in objection the one isolated passage in which He declared a limitation of knowledge, is quoted, I reply that limitless power admits the possibility of self-limitation. I do not profess to explain, but I am not prepared upon the one and only affirmation of limited knowledge, to base a doctrine of ignorance, when, in all other speech and teaching Christ claimed such Oneness with the Father as to enable Him to speak, never in the terms of doubt or speculation, but always in those of certainty and finality.

It will at once be recognized that holding this view of the Person of Christ, it is impossible for me to believe that He was in any sense ignorant. Therefore His attitude toward the Old Testament settles for me forever the question of its Divinity.

There is, however, yet another word to be said in this connection. Even if the theory of the Kenosis in the form to which I have referred is still maintained as true, the difficulty of Christ's attitude toward the Old Testament is not removed. He emphatically declared that He spoke nothing from Himself, but only the things which His Father gave Him to speak.

Now I am not proposing to suggest that if the attitude He maintained toward the Old Testament were a false one it was God's mistake. I do, however, declare that if His recognition of the Divine authority of the Hebrew Scriptures was sincere, then if these Scriptures are not of Divine authority He was either insincere, or grossly deceived, when He declared that all His teaching was Divinely authorized.

This view of Him is also impossible. He was sinless, and therefore truthful; therefore all He said was by the will of His Father; therefore the Old Testament Scriptures are Divine.

2. *Christ's Testimony after His Resurrection.* I presume it will be admitted that the theory of the Kenosis, already referred to, does not apply beyond the resurrection. We turn, then, with interest to what Christ said concerning the Old Testament Scriptures after the resurrection.

In the Gospel according to Luke we have the story of His walk to Emmaus, and of a subsequent appearing to the disciples, in which stories His references to the Old Testament occur. On the way to Emmaus, in order to the illumination of the doubting and almost despairing disciples, "beginning from Moses and from all the prophets, He interpreted to them in all the Scriptures the things concerning himself." Thus, after the resurrection, by actual exposition of the Old Testament writings He ratified what He had said in the course of His public ministry concerning them; "These are they which bear witness of me."

Again, in the midst of His assembled disciples, He declared that His suffering and resurrection, and the ultimate moral issues resulting therefrom, were in fulfilment of the things "written in the law of Moses, and the prophets, and the psalms." That reference to the Old Testament is absolutely inclusive, naming as it does the three divisions familiar to every Hebrew. "The law of Moses" was the inclusive name of the Pentateuch. "The prophets" was the name of the division including Joshua, Judges, the four books of Kings, and all the prophets except Daniel. "The psalms" was the name of the division including the psalter, and all that remained. These were the Scriptures of the Hebrews in the days of Christ, and these are the Scriptures of the Old Testament as now incorporated in our Bible. Thus Christ, after His resurrection, affirmed the authority of these books by declaring that His work was the fulfilment of their teaching.

In this matter of Christ's relation toward the Old Testament we are compelled to accept one of three conclusions:

a. He was ignorant.
b. He was infallible, but did not think it was important to change popular conceptions of the Divinity of the Old Testament.
c. He was infallible, and criticism is always wrong when its conclusions conflict with His attitudes.

As to the first, I have already given my reasons for believing it to be absolutely untenable. To what I have already said let me add, that if it could be proved that He was ignorant in these matters, it would be impossible to be sure of His infallibility at any point. It has been declared that He was scientifically fallible, but spiritually infallible. That is surely to suggest the possibility that science and things spiritual may be contradictory. It is too late in the day to make any such assertion. The age of the merely physical scientist has passed. Dr. Jowett, in an address from the chair of the Congregational Union several years ago, declared: "We are living in a time when a great and awful dawn is whitening above horizons which have been shrouded in twilight and night, and vast outlines of psychological truth are now appearing." Everyone will agree with the accuracy of this statement. Science today is recognizing the fact that behind matter there is something of which it is but a manifestation. Less than fifty years ago they declared that beyond the material there was nothing. Ages ago Job had declared, "He hangeth the earth upon nothing." The scientists of today are discovering the truth in that poetic statement. The final science is the knowledge of that mysterious something which men have designated nothing. In the words of Jesus, "This is life age-abiding, that they should know thee, the only true God, and him whom thou didst send, even Jesus Christ."

If this be true it is unthinkable that One spiritually infallible, that is, knowing perfectly the final science, should be scientifically fallible.

A child of His age He was, speaking in its simple language, but never inaccurately; condescending to its methods of expression, but never consenting to its false thinking. I believe, therefore, that when He, before and after resurrection, treated the Scriptures of the Old Testament as being of Divine authority, He set a seal upon them which I dare not break, and dare not disregard.

As to the second objection that He was infallible, but did not think it important to change popular conceptions of the Divinity of the Old Testament, I at once dismiss it as involving the view that He was content to allow men to remain in superstition which He could have dissipated by a word.

There is but a third alternative, and I accept it as the conviction of my life, and the inspiration of my ministry. I believe that Christ was infallible, and that whenever criticism questions the accuracy of His attitude, it is wrong, whatever its conclusion may be.

And now a final word. A generation ago Dr. Dale declared that the final battle of criticism would be fought around the Person of Christ. That battle is now in process. As at the beginning, so at the close, I decline to charge the men who differ from me with insincerity, or with lack of devotion to the Christ, as they see Him and know Him.

I do, however, most unhesitatingly affirm that the Christ presented in what is popularly known as "Modernism" is not the Christ of the New Testament.

I am convinced that sooner or later it will be well for all of us that we understand clearly that the true line of division between us is created by our attitude to the Bible.

Those who do not believe that it is the infallible Word of God must be left free to work out their own theory. In all probability theories would be the more correct word. I do not know. I am not proposing to accompany them, but am prepared to treat them with every consideration and respect so long as they refrain from bitterness, and from attempting to build the superstructure of their new religion upon the foundations laid by those who have believed in the Christianity of the New Testament.

The hour has surely come for the formation of a new covenant of such as accept the authority of the Christ of the New Testament, and therefore of the Bible, as final. In such a covenant there would be room for diversities of interpretation, but none for the destruction of the Scriptures.

To those of us who still believe in the Bible as the final and infallible Word of God, there remains the Christ of virgin birth, of virtuous life, of vicarious death, and victorious resurrection; and with all confidence we may go forward with our work of seeking and saving the lost. The victories of nigh two thousand years, which are also the victories of the present hour, will be continued.

PAUL'S ESTIMATE OF LIFE

IN THE history of the Christian church perhaps no man, upon whom the eyes of the world have been fixed, has so wondrously fulfilled in character and conduct the ideal of Christianity as did the Apostle Paul. Most of us will agree that he realized more fully than any man of his own time the purposes of God as revealed in Jesus Christ. His life and teaching have revealed the meaning and Christianity in a way accomplished by no other life or teaching. It is very interesting in his letter to the Philippians, one of his later epistles, to find him writing of himself, and yet of himself principally in the new life, which he had then been living for about three and thirty years. He writes with human tenderness, of human sensibilities, and human thoughts, while yet upon all there rests the light of the divine, and through all there is manifested the power that has taken possession of him.

In this epistle, written to his children in the faith at Philippi, it is very evident that he writes under the stress of circumstances. Not that circumstances are causing him one moment's anxiety, but they are such as to compel him to face the alternative possibilities which lie just ahead of him. It is while in this condition that he writes this letter and condenses into one swift burning sentence an epitome of Christianity as he has realized it: "To me to live is Christ."

To this man, all the marvelous unfoldings of the doctrine and scheme of redemption can be condensed and expressed in the simplest of words. He tells the whole story of his own experience of Christianity when he writes, "To me to live is Christ" (Phil. 1:21). To him Christianity is Christ.

> Christ! I am Christ! and let the name suffice you,
> Ay, for me, too, He greatly hath sufficed;
> Christ is the end, for Christ was the beginning,
> Christ the beginning, for the end is Christ.

This statement of the apostle's view of Christianity gathers force when we remember the circumstances under which he wrote it. He was a prisoner in the charge of the Praetorian guard. He was waiting, most probably, for the final word of the emperor, which should decide in which of two ways his pathway should lie. If the emperor's command be given, the apostle will tread the road through the door of his prison, through the city to the place of execution, and then, by one swift, sudden stroke, his life will end. He looks along that road and thinks of the possibility of traversing it. Then he looks in the other direction. Suppose that the emperor command that he be set at liberty. Then back to Philippi he will speed to see his children, and on to some new region to tell the same story and live the same life and win more trophies for Christ. He looks at these two roads stretching before him, and he says:

"To live — is Christ, and to die — is gain. I am in a strait betwist two. I desire to depart, and yet for your sakes I would tarry a little longer."

Life and death have lost their old significance to him, because there is one vision that fills the horizon whether he look this way or that. Here it is Christ, and there it is gain, and gain is Christ, and Christ is gain. There is no darkness but only light, for everywhere he sees the Master. That is Christianity.

Now, beloved, I want to take that estimate of Christian life and meditate upon it for a little while. Do not expect me to exhaust it, for in this text lie all the possibilities and potentialities of the Christian life.

"To me to live is Christ." What did the apostle mean? There are seven things which he might have meant. By these words he intended to say that:

1. *Christ was the author of his life.* It was as though he had written, "To me to live at all is Christ."

2. *Christ was the sustainer of his life.* "To me to continue to live is Christ."

3. *Christ was the law of his life.* "The conditions in which I live my life are summed up in Christ."

4. *Christ was the product of his life.* "To me to live is to reproduce Christ."

5. *Christ was the aim and influence of his life.* "To me to live is to lead men to Christ."

6. *Christ was the impulse of his life.* "To me to live is to be swept along under the compassion of the Christ."

7. *Christ was the finisher, the crown of his life.* "To me to live is at last to be what he is, and to find the crowning of all my manhood in him."

Christ the end, as Christ was the beginning. Christ the beginning, and therefore Christ the end. Whether this man looked back upon the past, at the present, or into the future, within or without, behind, above, or beyond to the consummation — wherever he turned his eyes, he saw Jesus only.

The first thought is that when Paul wrote these words, "To me to live is Christ," he meant to say, "Christ is the author of my life."

This man did not count that he had any life except the life which was named "Christ." He began to reckon his life only from the day when Christ was born within him through the power of the Holy Spirit. In the life of this man, there is one clean line, dividing it about at its center. Behind that line is the old life, the "old man," to which he so often referred, while on the other side of the line is the new life, the "new man." To Paul, the crossing of that line was something that went to the very depths of his being. It transformed him so that in looking back to the days when he became a new man in Christ, he said of the old days, "Old things are passed away." They had all vanished out of his sight. He took no account of anything that was behind him, and he said, "All things are become new," and in the new things he lived. The years that he spent on the earth, prior to the moment when Jesus found him, he did not reckon as worth speaking of for a single moment.

Was Paul not mistaken? Had not very much of value been crowded into the years before his conversion? Stop him for a moment and ask him:

"Paul, what do you mean by this? You lived a very remarkable life before you met Jesus of Nazareth. You had been brought up at the feet of Gamaliel. You had all the advantages of learning and religion. You had never been a profligate. Your life had been straight and pure, clean through. You were a Pharisee of the Pharisees, a Hebrew of the Hebrews. In all outward seeming, and what is infinitely more, in all inward sincerity, you had been a remarkable man."

"Perfectly true; but the things I counted gain, I now count but dross."

"Why?"

"In comparison with what I found, when Christ found me. When I turned my back upon the old, I did it forever, because my face was set toward the new."

I do not think this man ever had five minutes' questioning as to whether he ought to go back into that old life once a week for enjoyment, and live the new life all the remainder of the week as a duty. The old life *passed away,* and the new life opened before him bright with joy, thrilling with delights, expanding all the way.

The apostle's new life began when there shone a light round

about him on the way to Damascus. We learn so much by contrast. Look at him for a moment on the way to Damascus. Remember that he was straight, upright, moral, righteous, sincere to the core of his being; and on his way to Damascus he carried in his hand some very important documents — letters from the high priest. What for? Because in Damascus there was a little company of men and women who were daring to slight the religion of their fathers, singing hymns about this Jesus, whom the friends of Paul had crucified. If they should go on singing their hymns they would soon undermine the national religion, and Paul was going to put an end to it. So he was riding with the priest's letters in his possession, when a light from heaven fell, and a voice from heaven spoke. Paul fell to the ground, and the man upon the earth said in answer to the voice from heaven:

"Who art thou, Lord?"

The revelation that came to him must have been the most startling of his life: "I am Jesus whom thou persecutest."

Now hear the next word and never forget it:

"Lord!"

What a change! Why, this man has joined the church at Damascus before he arrives there! That is all they are doing, calling Jesus, Lord, and Paul has done it. Do you not see the radical nature of this change? Do you not see that he has taken the crown of his life from off his own head and has put it on the head of Jesus?

"Lord," — and what else? "What wilt thou have me to do?"

That is henceforth the keynote of his life. The music is true to it through all the future; through missionary journeyings, through perils by land and by sea, in prison and among robbers, when suffering persecutions or preaching the gospel of the grace of God, he is always true to the keynote which he struck when he said, "Lord, what wilt thou have me to do?" There his life began. There the old life dropped away, and the new life opened before him; and looking back to that beginning from the jail in Rome, he writes:

"To me to live is Christ."

Life began there, and we may judge how real the change was by asking him a question, which I often think I shall want to ask him when by God's grace I meet him in the glory:

"Paul, you have not forgotten the ride to Damascus?"

"No, I still remember the hour of my apprehending by the Lord."

"But, Paul, *what did you do with the high priest's letters?*"

Did you ever think of that? I shall want to know some day. They went clean out of his life like everything else of the old life. Old things passed away.

That is when Paul began to live. When is your birthday, my brother? Let me say something for the sake of those who say, "I cannot find my birthday." By a question like that, some trembling soul may be unsettled. The devil is only too glad to take hold of anything whereby he may unsettle any one. If the devil says to you, "You haven't had any birthday," treat him as I do and say, "If I never had one, I will have one now." If Satan is so very particular about a definite date, take this one and say to God right now:

> Here I give my all to thee,
>   Friends and time and earthly store;
> Soul and body, Thine to be,
>   Wholly Thine forever more.

The Master says, "Him that cometh unto me, I will in no wise cast out." We have the date, and any "now" will do; so we will dismiss the devil and pass on. The point is that there is a passing into the new life and a turning of the back upon the old. "To me to live is Christ." Blessed fact of regeneration, to which we owe everything that comes after it! All the new possibilities which God offers to us are the result of the fact that the

Master arrested us and gave us His life, so that old things passed away and all things became new.

But Paul means infinitely more. He means also, "To me to continue to live is Christ." Three and thirty years, or thereabouts, he has been following Jesus, and the music of his life has been running on amid earth's lamentations. The harmonies have been varied, but that has always been the chord of the dominant.

But what does he mean when he says that to him "to continue to live is Christ"?

It is a confession on the part of this man of his own helplessness. He says:

"Here I am after three and thirty years, by the grace of God. I am still living the same life that then began."

"But how?"

"Christ. I have not kept Him; He has kept me. I have not clung to the cross; the Man of the cross has clung to me, which is infinitely better. He has sustained my life during these three and thirty years."

Beloved in Christ, do we sufficiently grasp that great truth for ourselves? Weak, trembling men and women, who have started the Christian life, are crying and wondering how they will hold out. If it is left to you, I will not expect to meet you in the Christian pathway twelve months hence. If it is left to me, I will be a castaway very shortly.

You remember that wonderful figure from the lips of Jesus recorded in the Gospel by John. There Christ says that He is not only the author but the sustainer of life. "I am the vine, ye are the branches." Paraphrase that; put it into other words so as to bring out the inner thought. People have an idea that Jesus meant to say: "I am the main stem of the vine, and you are the branches grafted into me. Through me, the main stem, all the forces of life pass into you the branches."

That is very beautiful, but Jesus meant something infinitely stronger.

What did he say? "I am" — not the main stem — "I am *the vine.*" What is the vine? Root, main stem, branches, leaves, tendrils, fruit — everything. That is the vine. People speak as though the main stem alone was the vine, held up by roots and expressing itself in branches. That is true in a sense, but I like to take this word of Christ's in its sublimity. "I am the vine" — the whole of it. What does this mean? "Ye are the branches — part of the vine — and the life of the branch is the life of the vine." In a sense the vine gives its life to the branch, but not as a separate thing. The branch is part of the vine, and the very life that courses through the branch and reproduces itself in fruit is the life of the vine. "To me to live is Christ." His life it is, that sustains me. It is He Himself in me. I am His; He is mine. We are one by a solemn union, a union infinitely beyond anything that metaphor or figure can teach, one with each other, and by that fact of our oneness my life has been sustained. "To me to live is Christ."

I love this third thought: "To me to live is Christ. Christ is the condition of my life; Christ is the law of my life."

That is why Paul was angry with the Galatians. He said to them:

"O foolish Galatians, ye ran well; who hath hindered you?"

How did he say they had been hindered? They were getting back under legalism, into the place where they continually said, "Thou shalt not" and "Thou shalt"; and where they were bringing everybody up to the test of forbiddings and permissions, and asking for a rule for everything. Paul said:

"You ran well; what hath hindered you? How is it you are so soon entangled with the yoke of bondage?"

How is it with you, Paul?

"To me to live is *Christ;* not a set of rules, but a life principle within me; not the conditioning of my days by time-tables and maxims and rules, but the ever-present Christ stretching to the farthest territory of my being, and by His presence there ordering all my life within the bounds of His own sacred will."

Paul lived in the new covenant of which Jeremiah spoke, the covenant in which the law should be written no longer upon the table of stone outside a man's personality, but on his heart, so that if a man wanted to know what God would have him do, he need go to no temple, to no priest, to no altar, to no code of rules. He need but to turn himself to silence and quietness and say:

> O strong life of God in Christ within me,
> Direct, control, suggest this day
> All I design, or do, or say,
> That all my powers with all their might,
> In thy sole glory may unite.

The man that lived there had a fresh code of ethics every morning, a new list of regulations every moment; and all these came along the impulse of the Christ-life within him. Christ is the law of my life; He conditions my days; He is the author, the sustainer, and the law.

Again, it is as though this man had said: "Christ is the product of my life. To me to live *is* Christ."

But if a man says that, and there is no manifestation of it, who believes him? Not I. And I am quite sure that this man did not want any one to believe him unless it was perfectly evident in his life.

Suppose that here is a man living a life that is selfish and malicious and proud and critical and unkind, and he says:

"To me to live is Christ."

O man, do not blaspheme! Your life is selfish, your life is malicious, your life is critical, your life is unkind; was Jesus any of these?

"Oh, no," he says. "I do not mean that. I mean that I have accepted His creed."

Never! No man ever really accepted the creed who did not get the Christ first. The creed grows out of the living Christ; and when that is so, the creed is forever manifesting itself in conduct.

Do you not see, beloved, the necessity for this? Nature, so far as we understand it, always reproduces itself true to type. I remember the last season in which I put flowers in my garden in Birmingham, I went down to a shop and bought some bulbs, because I wanted a fine show of tulips in the earlier days of the year. I put them all carefully in my garden. I even arranged them according to a color scheme, and in geometrical precision. I almost dreamed of the result, for I love God's flowers, though I do not understand them. The winter went; spring came, and the bulbs came up, but they were crocuses. Why? Because I had planted crocus bulbs. I thought I had a bargain, and the result was, that what I had sowed that I reaped.

Now work out that great principle of life and apply to this question of sainthood. If the life implanted in you is the life of Christ, that must reproduce itself true to type. If a man has not quit singing, "I want to be an angel," he is on a sorry business, because he has not even a promise of wings anywhere on him. But if a man is singing reverently, with strong crying and tears and earnest desire, "I want to be like Jesus," that is possible. Why? Because the life he lives, if he is born again, is the Christ-life, and if the life of Christ be implanted within him, it will in its own outworking, reproduce itself, and he will, individually as well as with the church, grow up into Him in all things which is the head, even Christ.

Let us endeavor to understand this better by looking at two illustrations from Paul's life.

We saw him just now on the way to Damascus. I have the profoundest admiration for Saul of Tarsus before he was converted. I love a man who is sincere and out and out in anything. But do you see what Paul's sincerity did for him in those old days? It made him say, in effect:

"I am sincere, and I am determined that the religion of my God shall be *the* religion. If men will not bow to it, then I will hail them to prison, and to death. My sincerity arouses my indignation, and I am determined to smite to death the men who will not abide by that which is a divinely revealed religion."

There he is, a magnificent man, the best that human nature can ever do for a man apart from Jesus Christ. Do not forget it. There has nothing finer been brought out of fallen human nature than Saul of Tarsus before Christ found him.

Thirty years have gone, and now we see him before Agrippa and his friends, who desire to amuse themselves by looking at this strange man, and hearing what he has to say. Paul gives his testimony, tells the story of how Jesus found him and transformed him. Agrippa looking at him, said not, "Almost thou persuadest," but with scorn:

"With a very little would you persuade me to be a Christian?"

What does Paul say? Is he any less sincere and consecrated than he was when he rode to Damascus? No. Is he less enthusiastic? No. Is there any difference? Yes, a vast difference! How does he show it? Manacles are on his wrists, and chains upon his ankles, but he looks into the face of Agrippa and says:

"O King Agrippa, I wish that, not with a very little, but that altogether thou wast such as I am, except these bonds. I do not want you to wear my chains, Agrippa. Have my Christ, have my light, have my life, but I would not put these on even you, Agrippa."

Do you see any change in the man? Perfectly sincere thirty years ago, but if you did not agree with him he would put you to death. Perfectly sincere now, but with an entirely changed tone:

"O King Agrippa, if you could only change places with me

without having my chains; but I would not harm or pain you for a moment!"

If a man lives Christ, he reproduces Christ. Is not that what Paul has done? Are not his words the living echo of that most wonderous prayer of all, "Father, forgive them; they know not what they do"? Men always in some measure reproduce Christ when they live His life. If the Christ-life is present it must come out through the glory on the face, and the tenderness of the touch, and the new love for everybody. The very best testimony that you can ever give to the power of Jesus Christ is to live His life over again, not in your own effort, but by the propulsion of that same life within you. "For me to live is to reproduce Christ."

Let me mention the other points briefly. "To me to live is to influence men toward Christ. The *aim* of my life is Christ."

Do you think that many of those soldiers that were fastened to Paul got away without being influenced for Christ? I do not. Every soul he came into contact with was an opportunity; and all his life, so far as active service went, was poured out in the doing of this one thing: the bringing of men who had never seen the Christ into the place where they might see Him; and the building up of those who had seen Him in their most holy faith from height to height, and from glory unto glory. The whole aim and influence of his life was Christ.

Again, the *impulse* of his life was Christ.

I use the word "impulse" in reference to the great force behind it, which impelled him to service. Take one illustration. You know the epistle to the Romans — that is, you know where it is. Well, read it again. You have never fathomed it yet. I am just beginning to see light upon it, beauteous gleams of glory on it. Chapter 5, justification; 6, the question of sin; 7, that question still discussed; 8, no condemnation, the larger, purer life; 9, what there? Well, do not read the ninth without reading the last verses of the eighth. What is the highest height of experience in the eighth? "For I am persuaded that neither death, nor life, nor angels, nor principalities, nor powers, nor things present, nor things to come, nor height, nor depth, nor any other creature, shall be able to separate us from the love of God, which is in Christ Jesus our Lord."

I always think of the apostle here as on some mountain eminence, looking at his enemies. They are all around him — death, life, angels, principalities, powers, things present; and then his imagination sweeps him into all the infinite possibilities of the future — things to come, height, depth, or any other creation. There they all are, the possibilities of danger. He says, "I am persuaded that none of them shall be able to separate us from the love of God which is in Christ Jesus." There he is at the height of vision, the height of experience.

What next? "I say the truth in Christ, I lie not, my conscience also bearing me witness, that I have great heaviness and continual sorrow."

Why, 8:38, 39 do not sound like that! They are a shout of triumph, "Nothing can separate me from His love, but I have great heaviness and continual sorrow."

What about? About himself? No; self had perished in the struggle of these preceding chapters. What about? "I could wish that myself were accursed from Christ for my brethren, my kinsmen according to the flesh." What is that? That is, "To me to live is Christ. The impulse of my life is the Christ-impulse. The passion that brought Him down to redeem men, consumes me, and when I have touched the highest height of His life so that I know that nothing can separate me from His love, then I have learned the deepest experience of all, that of fellowship in His suffering, and I wish I could be accursed." Jesus Himself was made a curse for us, and Paul is living the Christ-life, so that he can say,

Oft, when the Word is on me to deliver,
 Lifts the illusion and the truth lies bare,
Desert or throng, the city or the river,

> Melts in a lucid paradise of air.
> Only like souls I see the folk thereunder
>   Bound who should conquer, slaves who should be kings,
> Hearing their one hope with an empty wonder,
>   Sadly contented in a show of things;
> Then with a rush the intolerable craving
>   Shivers throughout me like a trumpet call,
> Oh, to save these, to perish for their saving,
>   Die for their life, be offered for them all!

Let commentators cease their foolish attempts to explain away those verses. Paul has come nearer to Jesus Christ here than ever before. This impulse of the Christ-life which wrought redemption for the race at the cost of His own life enters a human soul, and floods it to overflowing, until he says:

"I could wish that even I were accursed for my brethren's sake."

What is the last thing? *Christ is the crown.* He is not only the author; He is the finisher. He not only began; He will end the good work.

And when it ends, what is it? Christ. What is the music of the land to come? Christ. What the fellowship? Christ, and Christ reproduced in the saints. What will be my chief joy when I look again in the face of my child who has gone before me and is to wait for me in the shining city? It will be that she is like Jesus. Not only shall we see Christ Himself, but Christ reproduced in the loved ones.

Imagination is sometimes ahead of truth. Poetry guesses at more than prose ever fathoms. Follow out the thought, and everywhere, on the throne, and amid the multitudes, what see you? Christ. That is why this man Paul stands and notwithstanding Nero's threatened axe, says:

"To die is gain."

"Do you not see that executioner, Paul?"

"No, I do not see him."

"What do you see?"

"Christ! To die is gain."

Now let me ask you to finish this theme for yourself. Imagine that you have in your hand a clean piece of paper, and write on it for yourself — God help you? — take the pencil and write! Write the story of your life, honestly, faithfully, truth, in as brief a sentence as Paul wrote the story of his. Write:

"To me to live is — money."

Now, be honest, in God's name. If you have played the hypocrite before, do not do it now. Write it down, not for man's eyes, but for God's. "To me to live is money." If that it true, put it down.

"To me to live is pleasure."

"To me to live is fame."

Oh, fill them in for yourself!

Now you have it written, your life's story. You never looked it squarely in the face like that before. There it is, right in front of you, the self-evident truth, the inner meaning of all your life.

Now finish it. Write under it what Paul did. That is your estimate of life; now add Paul's estimate of death:

"To me to live is money; to die is — I cannot write 'gain' after that. To die is *loss*. I shall leave it all. Naked came I out of my mother's womb; naked shall I return thereunto."

"To me to live is pleasure; to die — oh! do not talk to me about death! It is the last thing I want to think about. I want my pleasure, my laughter, this hollow crackling of thorns under a pot; 'tis all I have! Let me have it, but in God's name do not talk about death. Why, man, I do not like to walk down the street in the dark because I think of death. I cannot write that."

"To me to live is fame." Now, finish it. "And to die — no, I cannot. For if they put my name on a marble monument, directly it is erected, nature, with mossy fingers, will begin to pull it down. I cannot write that. To die is to perish, to be forgotten! What is fame when I am gone? I cannot write it."

No, beloved, and you cannot write Paul's estimate of death

after anything except Paul's estimate of life. If, by God's great grace, you can write, "To me to live is Christ," you can write, "To die is gain." To die is to see Him more clearly, to be closer to Him, to enter into larger service for Him, to touch the height and the depth and the length and the breadth of His life; "to die is gain." You can only write it if you write the first.

Somebody else says: "Well, I have never written the first; can I start?"

Yes.

"Where can I start?"

Where he started.

"Where did he start?"

"Lord, what wilt thou have me to do?" That is it. Will you say that?

"Yes, we will do it. Is it easy?"

No, it is not easy. The cross is there, crucifixion is there, the ending of self is there, the abandoning of everything, of hope, and wife, and child, and home, and friends, and ambition, all is there. "Lord — I have had other lords — Lord, I have been governed by self, I have been governed by human loves, I have been mastered by passions, I have been swept along by ambitions; Lord, Nazarene, depose these other lords and be King."

That is the place to begin; and there is not a man or woman who begins there honestly to whom He will not come with healing on His wings, the sun rising; then the old things for you shall pass away, and all things shall become new.

THE HIDDEN YEARS AT NAZARETH

THE SOUL'S first vision of Jesus is of Him as the Saviour. When we so know Him, He becomes to us the exemplar, leaving us an example, that we should follow in His steps. He is more than an example in any ordinary acceptation of that term, for He not only reveals to us the pattern of our lives, but He also bring the power by which we may grow up into Him in all things, and so reproduce in actual living the perfect and wondrous pattern that He shows. But we must clearly understand that we never get back into the life of Jesus save by the way of His death. His death is evermore the gate of life to man — not only a gate to the eternal life that stretches beyond this place and time of conflict, but the gate into the eternal life which we live today, if we are living in direct and positive communion with Himself. Having known Him as the Saviour, and having found our way into the realm of life at the cross, then He becomes our example, and all that He is in the revelation of the fourfold gospel marks His intention for His people.

Now, beloved, let us seek to learn the purpose of Christ for us in one particular department of life.

It is not given to every man or woman to serve God in public places; the great majority must live their lives outside any prominent sphere, and as part of a very small circle of relatives and acquaintances. Men will not hear even the names of the great mass of the people who are living their life throughout

the world today. I want to know what there is in the life
of Jesus that helps such persons. We are accustomed to think
of Him as one in a public ministry, as the man in the market-
place and the crowd, the teacher who "spake as never man
spake," the leader whose touch brought life and blessing to
hundreds, the man who rebuked sin in high places and spoke
words of infinitely sweet pity and kindness to the child and
the young disciple; but the greater part of His life was not
lived in those places where we have grown most familiar with
Him, but in quiet seclusion, where the great crowd of men
and women will always live in this world. Yet how little we
know concerning that period! how meager is the biblical information! I do not say it is enough; I believe it is enough;
but in the mere matter of words, how small it is! I have the story
of His birth, and then I lose sight of Him for twelve years. Then
I see Him again, going out to His Jewish confirmation, becoming the son of the law in that Jewish congregation, asking
questions of the doctors, and answering theirs. Ah, it is a wonderful glimpse, a glittering flash, and then I lose Him again
for eighteen long years, at the end of which time He comes
to be baptized of John in Jordan, and begins His public ministry,
and I see a few rapid pictures of miracles and tears and love
and sympathy, and He is gone! If you will write, in the manner
in which the lives of the men of today are written, the story
of the daily life of Jesus, how diminutive and meager it is!

What of those eighteen years? Where was He? What was
He doing? As one whom He has ordained to preach His gospel
in this public ministry, I am intensely interested in the way
He spoke to men and acted among men in His public years;
but the majority will feel that they would be better served by
a revelation of how He acted amid the commonplace surroundings of everyday life.

Let us, then try and see Him in those eighteen hidden years.
The two verses that I have read are the only two that give

us any definite or detailed account of what Jesus was doing from the time He was twelve until He was about thirty. Take the two statements and fix them on your minds for a moment: "Thou art my beloved Son, in whom I am well pleased." "Is not this the carpenter?" These two passages supply the story of the eighteen years. Jesus was a carpenter pleasing God. But is it fair to put them together like that? I think you will see that it is. Upon what occasion did that divine voice speak? On the occasion of the baptism. Jesus had left behind all the doings of those long and weary years, and He was just at the dividing line between private and public life. He was leaving behind Him the unknown years, and coming out into the fierce light that beats ever upon a public teacher. And there, at the parting of the ways, God lit up all the years that had gone with the sweet words of approval, "Thou art My beloved Son, in whom I am well pleased." It could not have been a pronouncement upon the temptation of the wilderness, that was as yet an untried pathway. It could not have been a declaration of the divine pleasure with Gethsemane's garden and Calvary's cross; they were still to be reached. No; it must have been a reference to the past, so that, whatever else I know, or do not know, about the hidden years of the life of Jesus, this one thing is certain, that through them all He pleased God; for God put His seal upon them when they were closing behind Him and the new years were opening before Him, saying: "I am well pleased." You remember how, after that pronouncement, He went to the wilderness and was tempted, and after that temptation He went to Galilee, in the power of the Spirit, and began His public ministry; and you find Him going at the early part thereof down to Nazareth, the place where He has been brought up. It was a small town, a kind of hamlet on the hillside, of perhaps three thousand inhabitants.

This young man comes back to His boyhood's home, and every one knows Him. He goes to the synagogue, as was His custom, on the Sabbath day, and reads out of the book, and then He talks to the assembled people; and they look at Him, and listen, wonder the while being depicted on their faces. Cannot you see the picture? — that little synagogue, the old Jewish people, the keen faces looking at the speaker, and then turning to each other, saying: "Whence hath this man these things? We know Him perfectly well; He is the carpenter." Yes; they know Him. They have watched Him toiling day after day, month after month, in the workshop, bending over the bench with the tools of His craft in His hand. They cannot account for Him as a teacher because they did not account for Him as a toiler.

Mark, then, what these people said about Him. Other men made the blunder of saying He was the son of the carpenter; but these men, by a sudden flash, light up for us the eighteen years by saying, "Is not this the carpenter?" I have now two facts concerning this period. I have the testimony of the men who knew Him best, and the testimony of God, who knew Him better than they did. Let us first take the human declaration, "Is not this the carpenter?" and hold it in the light of the divine, "In whom I am well pleased"; and then let us take the divine revelation, "Thou art my beloved Son," and hold it in the light of the human, "Is not this the carpenter?"

I do not want to hide the majesty of this sweet word the "carpenter" by any multiplication of words of mine. If any of you paint pictures, have you not sometimes been annoyed at the way in which men have framed them? You invite your friends' attention to a work of art, and they exclaim, "What a lovely frame!" and do not seem to see the picture. We sometimes frame the picture of God's words in like manner. Let us express ourselves so that the picture is seen and not the frame. "Is not this the carpenter?" For the greater part, then, of the life of Jesus, He worked with His own hands for His own living. That brings the Son of God, in living, pulsating life, close to every man who works. There is a beautiful tradition, that Joseph, His reputed father, died while Jesus was yet a child, and so He worked not merely to earn His own living, but to keep the little home together in Nazareth, and Mary and the younger members of the family depended upon His toil. That is a beautiful tradition. It may be true, but I do not press it. But I do press this upon you above everything else, that *He worked for His living.* Oh, that we could get all the strength and comfort which this fact is calculated to afford! Business men, you who have been at work all the week and have been harassed by daily labors and are weary and tired and seeking for new inspiration, this Jesus, whose name has become a name of sweetness and love, was not a king upon a throne, He was not for the greater part of His life a teacher with the thrill and excitement of public life to buoy Him up. No, the long years ran on and He was doing what some of you speak of as "the daily round, the common task." The man Jesus rose at daybreak, and, picking up His tools, made yokes and tables in order that He might have something to eat, and that, not for a brief period, but for eighteen years. He was an apprentice boy, a young man improving His craft, a master in His little shop with the shavings round Him and the tools about Him. That is the human picture. But that human picture becomes supremely precious to me as the light of the divine falls upon it. The eighteen years are over, the tools are laid aside, His feet will no more make music as He walks among the rustling shavings. God says, "I am pleased." It may have meant that God was pleased with Jesus because in those years He lived in the realm of the spiritual rather than the material. I believe it did mean that, but I am not going to dwell upon it. It may have meant that He was careful to think of, and pray for, and teach the younger members of His household, or that He was regular in His attendance upon the services of the synagogue. I think it did mean that, because I read, "He went to the synagogue, as was His custom, on the Sabbath day." But I want to know what God meant about the shop, and I am going to suggest to you two things. In the first place — and you will forgive this way of putting it, because I want the truth of it to abide upon your hearts, and if the phrasing be not elegant I want it to be forceful — it meant that Jesus had never done in that carpenter's shop a piece of work such as we speak of in the closing years of the nineteenth century as being "shoddy work." "I am pleased." God could not have been pleased with carpentry that was scamped any more than with blasphemous praise. "I am pleased," and every bit of work has on it the light of divine truth. When Jesus sent out from that carpenter's shop yokes that the farmers would use, they were so fashioned and finished that they would gall no ox. "Take my yoke upon you" gathers force and strength as an illustration from the fidelity of the carpenter's shop. When Jesus said, "Take my yoke," it was because He knew that it would not gall, it would be finished and perfect. Sometimes we have overshadowed the carpenter's shop with Calvary's cross. We have no right to do it. We have come to forget the fidelity of the Son of God in the little details of life as we have gazed upon His magnificent triumphs in the places of passion and conflict. In the second place, the divine approval meant that the influence of the life had been pure and bright and good. You all know the effect of influence. What sort of influence has He exerted? Pure and strong! I have sat sometimes in meditative mood, and thought of my beloved Lord, and tried to carry myself back, with all the interests that are nearest to my heart, into that land and that time when He was on earth, and I have thought, if I could just have taken my boy and apprenticed him to that carpenter, what a blessed thing it would have been. I do not think Jesus would have given him Psalm 119 to learn before he came to work in the morning, or have been talking to him forevermore about heaven and getting ready for it, and hell and shunning it. But he would have lived a bright, strong, glad life before Him, for no life ever touched the life of the Son of God but was the brighter and purer and stronger for the contact; and so, when the years of the carpenter's shop are over, God sets His seal of appoval upon them, first, because the work has been well done; and, secondly, because the influence of the life has been true and right and noble.

Who is this coming up out of the waters of baptism, upon whom the dove hovers and settles, and concerning whom heaven's voice is heard to speak? God marks Him out here from all His fellowmen. "Thou art my beloved Son." Not "Thou art a son, a child of mine," but "my Son." And, to the Hebrew mind, that links Him with all the prophecies of the past. He is the anointed of God. He is the one personage who is charged with the great mission of restoring the kingdom of God. God marks Him in that great word as His appointed Messiah, as Shiloh, as the Daysman from on high, as the Dayspring; all the wondrous words of past prophecy are settled upon Him, and God marks Him as the anointed One for the carrying out of the great scheme of redemption for the human race. And now He is standing on the banks of the Jordan, and we look upon Him for the first time with amazement and astonishment, and wonder, if this be the beloved Son of God, what has He been doing, where has He been in the years preceding this public manifestation? Come back again to the question, "Is not this the carpenter?" and the wonder is presented in a new vision, from a new standpoint, from another side. The Son of God, charged with the greatest commission that any being in heaven or earth has ever had to bear, was for eighteen years at work in a carpenter's shop. Now, we hardly see the wonder of this thing until we look more closely at it. I may be speaking to some young man upon whose heart is lying the burden of India, the need of China; he is travailing in spirit, even in this favored land, for the dark masses of Africa;

he is touched with the sacrificial passion of the Son of God to go and save somebody, and yet God has shut him up here at home. He has to live and care for a sick one. He cannot go. The fire is there, but the door is not open. The passion for men consumes him, but God shuts him out from service. Now, it is only those who know something of what that experience is who can understand the strange marvel of the Son of God, commissioned to do the work that precedes your passion, the infinitely greater work, holding in its grasp and love all the enterprises for the uplifting of man. And yet with that passion upon Him, with the cross ever before Him and His ultimate triumph in front, every morning He goes to the carpenter's shop, every day He does work, every night goes home to rest. I tell you it is a mystery of mysteries to us restless spirits. What does it mean? How is it that He, the beloved of God, the anointed of God, can be — there is no irreverence in saying it — content? Now, the answer is here. Jesus lived in the power of the truth, which we are so slow to learn, that there is something infinitely better than doing a great thing for God, and the infinitely better thing is to be where God wants us to be, to do what God wants us to do, and to have no will apart from His — to be able to say:

> I worship Thee, sweet will of God,
>   And all Thy ways adore!
> And every day I live, I seem
>   To love Thee more and more.

Jesus understood that. The carpenter's shop was the will of God for Him, and therefore He abode in that shop and did the work incidental to it. Now, pray do not misunderstand me. From the illustration I used a moment ago, you come to think that I intend to say Jesus did it as a duty while He longed for the cross. Nothing of the kind. "I delight to do thy will, O my God." Go and ask Him, talk with Him reverently across the distance of nineteen hundred years. "O Nazarene, where wouldst Thou rather be today, here among this work, or among the crowd, healing and teaching, and preaching to them?" and the answer would be, "God's will for me is in the carpenter's shop, and therefore that is the place of my joy." But I am going to ask you to press this question a little further. Was this a capricious matter, this will of God for Jesus? Does it not look hard and arbitrary that God should have put that saintly soul to such common labor? Why not have let Him face the conflict and get the victory, and hie Him back to heaven? There was a deep necessity in the whole arrangement. Let me put it superlatively, and say, Calvary's cross would have been nothing but the tragic ending of a mistaken life, if it had not been for the carpenter's shop! In that carpenter's shop He fought my battles. My hardest fight is never fought when there is a crowd to applaud or oppose, but when I am alone. Now, that was what Jesus was doing for eighteen years. There was no crowd to sing "Hosanna"; no other crowd to cry "Crucify him"; but alone He did His work and faced all the subtle forms of temptation that beset humankind, and one by one He put His conquering foot upon the neck of them, until the last was baffled and beaten, and His enemies were palsied by the strong stroke of His pure right arm. That is what He was doing. There was necessity for it, and because of Nazareth's shop there came Gethsemane's garden and Calvary's cross, and so, abiding in the will of God, by victory upon victory. He won His final triumph, and so opened the kingdom of heaven to all believers.

Now, beloved, from this study what are we to learn? I can only write off for you, very briefly, one or two lessons, and the first is a relative lesson. I never come back to this story of the early years of Christ, and read what these men of Nazareth said about Him, without learning how dangerous a thing it is to pronounce my little sentence upon any single human life. O men of Nazareth, down in that carpenter's shop that you pass and repass, where you sometimes pause and look in and see Him at His work, there is the One who spoke and it was done, who put His compass upon the deep, who fashioned all things by the word of His power, and you have never seen Him and never known Him, and your estimate of Him is that He is one of you — only a carpenter. Job's judges and Christ's critics are on a level, and they are on a level with every one of us who tries to pass his sentences upon his fellow men. If people ask you for your explanation of the mysterious circumstances of a brother man, tell them it is a mystery of God; for the moment you suggest that there was something wrong somewhere you may be getting into the region of blasphemy. Perhaps that man has been broken on the wheel by the Potter for a remaking. "If the Potter break the wheel, he shall remake it"; and God's fairest, highest place of service in the land that lies beyond will be filled by the men and women who have been broken upon the wheel on earth. Do not let us forget that, and if we cannot understand what God is doing with that woman whose heart is crushed and broken with overwhelming sorrow, let us be reverently silent, lest we help the men who drive the nails, and break the Lord's own heart.

But I gather not only this relative lesson; there are personal lessons. The first is this: the phrase "common task" should be struck out of every life. Jesus taught us that all toil is holy if the toiler be holy. Not for the sake of controversy, but as a protest against the misconception of human life, I tell you that no man has any right, simply because he preaches or performs certain functions, to speak of himself as a man in "holy orders." The man who goes out to work tomorrow morning with his bag on his back and his tools in it, if he be a holy man, has claims to that distinction; and if that man go down into the carpenter's shop and saw a piece of timber, the saw is a vessel of the sanctuary of God, if the man is a priest who uses it. All service is sacred service. I want you to carry this thought of the working Christ into all the days of the coming week, behind the counter and in the office, and, beloved sisters, if I may say so, in the home. Remember that George Herbert had caught the very spirit of this lovely thought when he sang of the possibility of sweeping a room and "making that and the action fine." Oh, if we could but get the Christian church, to say nothing of the outside world, free from the stupid and false ideas that this kind of work is honorable, and that is not, what a long way we should be on the road to the millennium! If every business man wrote his letters as though Jesus would have to look over them, what lovely letters we should have! I do not know that they would have tracts in them — that is not my point — but they would be true, robust, honest letters. O you business men, will you do your business for Christ, realizing that the work you do may be as sacred as my work? Sisters, will you take the home and make it a holy place for the shining of the Shechinah? If Christ lived the larger part of His life working, then our work is smitten through and through and lit with a new beauty, and we write over it, "Part of God's work for uplifting man."

I learn this lesson also, that no man is fit for the great places of service who has not fitted himself by fidelity in obscurity. You want, you tell me, to preach the gospel in China. Are you living it at home? God does not want men or women to preach His gospel anywhere who have not made it shine in their own homes. I do not ask, "Can you do the great work that hangs upon your hearts?" but, "Are you doing the present work faithfully?" Are you an Endeavorer, do you belong to the missionary society, that branch or this branch of the church, and are you so anxious to get to the meetings that you rob your master of even five minutes of his time? Christ does not count the service, but the five minutes you have stolen. What we want is to feel that if we are to do a big thing in the public service, we must be through and through true in the small things of life. The carpenter's shop made Calvary not a battle-field merely, but a day of triumph that lit heaven and earth with hope; and if you and I would triumph when our Calvary comes, we must triumph in the little things of the common hours.

BUT ONE THING

O N OLD Spanish coins there may be seen the two pillars of Hercules with the surrounding motto, *Ne Plus Ultra* ("No more beyond"). These coins were issued in the days when Spain was a great, and perhaps the greatest of the world powers. Possessing both shores of the Mediterranean, and imagining that she possessed all, she stamped her coins with these pillars, and engraved around them this motto.

But Columbus was born, and the passion of discovery being in him, he found that which lay beyond the pillars of Hercules; and Spain, still leaving those pillars upon her coins, changed the motto that surrounded them by cancelling the negative; so that on coins of later date the words *Plus Ultra* ("More beyond") are to be found.

This is a parable of what we are perpetually doing in life, looking forward to some limit, some ending, some goal, placing there the pillars of Hercules, writing round about them the line "No more beyond." As we approach the limit, we find light from beyond breaking upon us. We see lying on the other side of what we had thought of as a consummation and completion, vistas of things unknown and undiscovered. We are perpetually compelled to cancel some negation, and to say, as we look out through the pillars, "More beyond." In the days of training and preparation we are all apt, especially in the earlier part of them, to put the pillars of Hercules at the end of that process, to imagine that there is nothing beyond. We work, and toil, and labor toward the day of graduation; but we very soon discover as we approach this ending, that it is but sommencement, the beginning only, and we are compelled to cancel the negation that we placed at the front of our motto when we entered upon our work in school or college. Our motto is necessarily changed from *Ne Plus Ultra* to *Plus Ultra*. And it is this "more beyond" that is of supreme importance.

In order to ultimate realization, nothing is so important as a definite conception and a clear scheme. If these may but be gained, then all the thousand strands that lie across the pathway of the future may be taken up, and woven into the strong cable; but if we have no goal, no conception of the meaning of things, no great ideal, no overwhelming, all-inclusive passion, then we shall play with the strands and break them, and at the last have neither strands nor cable.

It is, therefore, my desire to say some words in order to help towards a true view of the ultimate, for the immediate must ever be set in the light thereof, if there is to be perfection of achievement; and if the true meaning and value of the immediate is to be understood.

No second, ticked off by the clock, has all its meaning in itself. It is a prophecy, a potentiality, a something that contains within itself an unexpressed meaning. Beyond the commonplace seconds as they pass — like seedlings which seem to be devoid of form and beauty, yet in every one of which there lies the making of the flower and fruit — is the ageless life which depends on them. Unless we have some conception of the ultimate, we shall indeed miss the meaning of the immediate.

As an interpreter of life, and an exponent of its true philosophy no greater has existed among human teachers than Paul, the apostle to the Gentiles. He occupies a throne of intellectual supremacy and spiritual power today, unchallenged notwithstanding the passing of the centuries. And in his writings he has strangely and wondrously revealed himself; the reason being that Paul did not preach a doctrine which was a doctrine merely, a theory which might be discussed wholly as a theory. He talked out of life. It has been said that Paul did not study theology in order to preach, but he studied his theology by preaching. Declaring the facts of the gospel, out of the experiences of his own life there came to him the true meaning and method of the gospel. You cannot study the writings of Paul without discovering revelations of his inner life. A little book called *St. Paul*, compiled, as the title-page tells us, by a deaconness, and having on the title page that word of Agrippa to him, "And Agrippa said unto Paul, Thou art permitted to speak for thyself," consists of a selection of these utterances of the apostle which reveal himself. It is without note or comment. The apostle speaks for himself.

Of these revealing sentences, the third chapter of the Philippian epistle contains the most interesting and fullest declarations. In this chapter we see him looking back, and looking forward, and then telling us the story of the present condition of his mind, of his heart, of his soul. His back is turned to the past, and his face is towards the future, and he declares in the phrase of the text what is the present attitude of his life, "but one thing!" This attitude is created by the vision that lies before him, and expressed in the fact that he has turned his back upon everything else. The passage as it stands in the original has a poetic sweep, which is somewhat obscured in the arrangement of our translation. I am not criticizing the translation for a moment, but I venture to read you the passage in the form in which Paul wrote it, leaving the peculiar formation and idiom of the language to make its own impression. In this way I think we catch the poetry and the passion which is very largely lost in the rearrangement of our translation.

"Brethren, I myself reckon not to have laid hold; but one thing — the things behind forgetting, and to the things before forthreaching — towards the goal I pursue, for the prize of the supernal calling of God in Christ Jesus."

That graphically describes the apostle's attitude. "I myself reckon not to have laid hold; but one thing" — the translators have here inserted the words "I do," and thus have weakened the passion of the statement. It is not only one thing I do, but one thing I am, one thing I have, one thing I see, one thing I think. It is all there. "But one thing — the things behind forgetting, towards the things before forthreaching, I press towards the goal of the supernal calling of God in Christ Jesus." Paul has also his pillars of Hercules. Whatever he wrote over them in those days in which his chief boast was that he was "a Hebrew of Hebrews," in those wonderful days when he could say even as concerning morality "as touching the righteousness which is in the law, found blameless," now he has written over them, not merely "More beyond," but "Everything beyond." "The things behind forgetting"; the things of today are pressed into the service of the passion of reaching out after the things of the future; everything beyond, "towards the goal I press for the prize of the supernal calling of God in Christ Jesus."

We confine ourselves to that central declaration, that great flash, which illuminates for us the apostle's heart and mind, and gives us to see what his conception of life really was. "But one thing." Will you then consider with me two things within the one thing: first, the impelling motive of this man's life, the "one thing"; and secondly, the resulting attitude of that motive, "But one thing."

First, the impelling motive. Now what did the apostle mean when he wrote this? What does it reveal of the man's inner life? May I at once summarize and say, first, it was the cry of illumination, "but one thing" — declaring the man's passion for final perfection. And yet again it was the sigh of limitation, declaring the man's impatience of present imperfection. And finally, it was the word of dedication, declaring the man's devotion to the immediate opportunity.

But now take the first. It was the cry of illumination. There is noticeable here a passion for final perfection. "But one thing."

Let me omit the phrases, "the things behind forgetting, and to the things before forth-reaching," and read straight on. "Brethren, I myself reckon not to have laid hold; but one thing... towards the goal I pursue." "I pursue," towards what? "Toward the goal of the on-high calling," or, as some have given it, "of the upward calling," or, better still, "of the supernal calling." That is the vision which he has seen through the pillars of Hercules, and which has made him cancel all negations; and in the passion of his soul for the realization of that, he devotes himself to the present.

What is that vision Paul has seen? He speaks of it as the "on-high calling of God in Christ Jesus." The vision seen was the vision of the on-high calling. Nothing can be more awkward than this phrase, the "on-high calling," and "the upward calling" does not give the true meaning. In the Latin Version this has been translated *"superna vocatio,"* the supernal vocation, not superior merely, but supernal. It is the vision and vocation of the upper things, not merely superior, but supernal, those which have to do with the infinite space beyond.

That great finality, the goal of life, what is it? We might discuss it here by considering the character and the conduct toward which the apostle looked, but we can most safely and perfectly answer and understand the question by saying it is Christ. Paul has seen Christ, and seeing Him he has seen the possibility of his own life. This explains the contrast and the choice he makes between old and new. I wonder if any other man has been able to write what Paul did, as to what he was before this vision broke upon his soul. "If any man have cause for boasting in the flesh," he says, "I more." And then he gives us the line of his boasting in the flesh. "Of the stock of Israel, of the tribe of Benjamin, a Hebrew of the Hebrews; as touching the law, a Pharisee; as touching zeal, persecuting the church; as touching the righteousness which is in the law, found blameless." I have the profoundest admiration for this man before he was a Christian. The whole caliber of his mind, and the makeup of his personality, the passionate earnestness that made him the avowed enemy of Christ is infinitely more satisfactory than much of so-called Christianity in the world today. My profound conviction is that every man ought to fight Christ or crown Him. Christ stands before the ages, making such claims and uttering such words, that He is either the profoundest imposter that ever crossed the ages, or He is all we have claimed for Him. We have yielded ourselves to Him because we have recognized this claim, and Paul was honest and sincere, fighting or crowning, crucifying or being crucified with, making to suffer or having fellowship with His sufferings. I look at this man before the vision, absolutely honest, sincere, devout, passionate, earnest, moral, and upright; a man of culture and learning. And yet he says, "The things that were gain to me I counted loss, I did count them but refuse" — no word is too strong for him to use to describe the worthlessness of these things to him, because the vision is so glorious. The vision of Christ has revealed to him the possibilities of his own being. He has seen in Christ what God's purpose is for him, for Paul. In the glorious beauty of the vision that broke upon him on the road to Damascus, he saw the thought of God for himself. Down into the deeps of the Infinite Love of the Infinite Heart he looked that day; and he found that he could be as that One was, the vision of whom blinded and apprehended him. Nay, he knew that his apprehension was in order that he might apprehend the One who apprehended him. He saw that he had been laid hold of, in order that he might lay hold of Him. He saw that the purpose of the revelation was that at last he might come out of that old life into something worthy. The vision seen, the supernal vocation broke upon him as a great revelation.

But I venture to think that was only part of the truth. I think the other truth lies within it. Not only was the vision seen, but the virtue was felt. It was the upward calling of God. Christ had not only been revealed to him — to quote the apostle's own words — Christ had been "revealed in him." Not only the ideal, the sight that had captured the mind, but a dynamic that was beginning the great and gracious work of changing the will and law of life under the touch of its constraining power. The call was supernal, it was the upward calling, not only the vision of the consummation, but also the attraction towards that finality. In the heart of the man there ever sounded the call. In the consciousness of the man there thrilled and throbbed the energy, reaching out, stretching on, approximating toward that final purpose which had so taken hold upon his soul.

The vision seen, Christ revealed to him: the virtue felt, Christ realized within him, what then? The victory is desired, and there grows within him the personal passion, the new consciousness, and he says: "Brethren, I count not to have laid hold; but one thing — the things behind forgetting, and to the things before forthreaching, I pursue towards the goal."

And yet is not this also the sign of limitation? If Paul has seen the vision of Christ, and felt His virtue, and so desires the victory, these very things create the consciousness of the present imperfection. He says: I have not already attained, I am not already made perfect. I have not yet laid hold. This is the constant consciousness of such as know anything of the Christ. Find me a man who tells you that he has now realized all there is for him in Christ, and I will show you a man who has lost his vision of the Christ. While the great light of the Christ vision beats upon the soul, it becomes increasingly conscious of imperfection, distance, constraint, limitation. Let me give you one of the paradoxes of Christianity. The nearer to

Christ, the further from Him. The nearer I press to His heart, the more am I conscious of the infinite distance that lies between Him and myself. The apostle says, "I have not yet laid hold, but one thing," and behind the "one thing" I catch, not only the cry of illumination, but also the sigh of limitation. And yet these two things acting together form the great power.

Yet again, it is the word of dedication, of devotion to the present opportunity. And now we may for a moment consider these phrases.

"But one thing — the things behind forgetting." Forgetting what? All those things of which he had boasted in his past. All those, and yet more. Forgetting what? The blessings behind. Never forgetting them in the sense of thankfulness for them, but never so living today as though the things of yesterday were of value. They had a value, but it has passed, to be forgotten. I shall best illustrate what I mean by saying, How many Christian people are living in the memory of a blessing received yesterday, ten, twenty, forty years ago? They were converted there, and then, and so, and you are quite surprised, for there are no evidences of the conversion present today. But they are living in the memory of the thing behind. "Forgetting the things behind." The Christ of yesterday will not suffice for me today, save as the Christ of yesterday is the Christ of today. If I am living in the memory of what He did on the way to Damascus, then I shall wander, for Damascus lies far behind on the pathway. Forgetting! Some men are always telling you how well they ran the race. Your best running in the past is nothing if you are slackening in the race now. "One thing!" "One thing — forgetting the things behind, and forthreaching to the things before — toward the goal I press." I persecute. But it cannot be that! It is exactly that. It is exactly the same word that he uses before when he says, "I persecuted the church." It does not mean persecuting here in the sense it did before; but it is the same word in the Greek — the same thought, the same intention, the same value, revealing the same attitude. I pursued the church; I pursue towards the goal. I followed the church like a hound upon the track; I press my way toward the final goal like a hound upon the track, with strong and passionate desire. All I was, as a persecutor of the church, I am today as I press toward that final goal. This man knew nothing of dilettante Christianity, he knew nothing of being

> Carried to the skies,
> On flowery beds of ease.

So fair and glorious were the visions that broke beyond the pillars of Hercules, that he panted as he pressed on, persecuting his way towards the great and glorious goal.

"But one thing," the cry of illumination, a passion for final perfection. He had seen the vision, and felt the virtue, and realized the victory. "But one thing," the sigh of limitation, an impatience of his present imperfection. "But one thing," the word of dedication, he pressed, he pursued toward the goal, with all the energy that characterized him in the days when he persecuted the church.

And now, secondly, if this is the hidden secret that lies behind that wonderful development of the apostle's life, shall we dwell relatively upon the statement, and ask, What is the resulting attitude?

I am venturing to commend this view and vision and ideal of life to those of you who are going out through the pillars of Hercules into a larger life. What effect will such a conception have upon life? Let me attempt to answer. First, that of a great narrowness; secondly, that of an infinite breadth; and finally, an issue much to be desired.

A great narrowness? Yes, let us at once say so. Let there be no mistake about this. We cannot accept these conceptions without becoming narrow. I do not hide it. I have no desire to hide it. "Narrow is the gate, and straitened is the way."

These words are sounding in our ears today, and they are the words of the infinite Master Himself. Do not let us try to escape them. Do not let us be swept away by desire into a false breadth that issues finally in the narrowness of destruction. These are the words of Christ. Said He, "Broad is the way that leadeth to destruction," and the word for destruction very literally means something imprisoned, confined, narrow. "Broad is the way," but notice, "it leadeth to destruction." But now hear Him once again. "Narrow is the gate, straitened is the path, but it leadeth to life." You commence with narrowness, but you pass out into the infinite spaciousness. You begin with the narrow gate and the straitened way, but they lead you into the large room. Narrowness — "but one thing"; breadth — life!

What kind of narrowness is this? It is the narrowness of exclusion, the narrowness that will compel men to "lay aside every weight, and the sin that doth so easily beset," the narrowness that will find no excuse for anything lingering in the life that blurs that great and glorious vision, a narrowness that will hurl out of the life those things which hinder the soul pressing toward the goal. If any one shall tell you that the way of an out and out devotion to Christ is the way of narrowness, doubt it not. It is the way of the narrowness of exclusion.

Yet it is the narrowness of consistency. And by the use of the word "consistency" I am not referring to much of the boasted consistency of some. The only consistent men in Christ's time in that sense were the Pharisees. I care nothing for that particular kind of consistency. You hear men say, I believe today exactly what I believed twenty-five years ago. I hate that kind of consistency, the consistency of a mere mental narrowness. Consistency is the power of holding together. Things consistent are things that hold together. The narrowness of the apostle was the narrowness of a great consistency, which issued eventually in the breadth of a great diffusion. There is a river so broad that it loses itself in the sands of the desert. There is a little brook, so narrow that it becomes broad and bears burdens upon its bosom. It is the narrowness of a great consistency, the narrowness which holds things together.

Therefore it is the narrowness of a great power. There are some things that must be narrow in order to be powerful. If you would drive an aperture into some hard substance, you must have a narrow instrument wherewith to do it. A knife must have a narrow edge to be of use. It is the narrowness of the river that creates its power, until presently breadth is accompanied by depth. When the river is so anxious to be broad as to forget depth, it is lost. It is the narrowness which issues in power.

And yet it is not narrowness merely, this Christian conception of life. It is breadth. "But one thing" — breadth, a breadth in the one thing, the new vision. How true it is that some people see so little. They are so narrow, and yet they are looking. Some of you remember that couplet D. L. Moody used to love to recite —

> Two men looked out from prison bars,
> One saw mud, and one saw stars.

That is a comparison of narrow and broad vision. You can look out today through your pillars of Hercules. and see mud or stars. It was a boy in an American class in an American school who, when his teacher had been at infinite pains to teach him about the sun, and the moment came when the teacher said, "Now, can you tell me what the sun is?" replied, "The sun is the thing that has spots on it." That is all some men know about it. This man Paul saw the stars and not the mud. "One thing." It was because he fixed his vision upon it that all the glory broke upon the soul. "But one thing."

And yet once more. Not merely a breadth of vision — and here I want to say very few words, and yet to be particular —

but the breadth of the things included in the one thing. I hope I have not made you think that Christianity is narrow in any single sense. Go over now to the fourth chapter of this particular letter to the Philippians. You never know all a person says in a letter until you come to the end of the letter. "Finally, brethren, whatsoever things are *true,* whatsoever things are *honorable,* whatsoever things are *just"* — but let us alter the emphasis here — *"Whatsoever things* are pure, *whatsoever things* are lovely, *whatsoever things* are of good report, if there be any virtue, and if there be any praise, think on *these things."* The word "think" here signifies to take account of, to make an inventory of, to count on. The apostle has included in that list all things essentially noble in thought and life, the true things, the honorable things, the just things, the pure things, the lovely things, the things of good report; of these he says take an inventory. Paul said "but one thing"; but now he says "things" — things, plural. But these *"things"* are never really possessed until "one *thing"* is possessed. It is when the soul has seen the vision of one thing that the other vision breaks in infinite light. Have the one thing, and you have everything. Lose the one thing, and the color will pass from the morning of your sky, everything you have dreamed of will fade. The breadth of the one thing is found in the all things possessed. Yet let the Master say the last thing. "Narrow is the gate, straitened is the way, but it leadeth unto life."

And what was the issue of this in the case of this man, the issue of this narrowness, the issue of this breadth?

First, he made a contribution to the world's enrichment for which the world is in his debt until this hour. I love to think of him, that man of weak bodily presence, that little man, that afflicted man; and yet if once you had begun to talk to him, you would have forgotten the weakness and smallness in the mighty sweep of his intellect, and the breadth of his spiritual teaching. I like to think of him making tents in Corinth until

Titus brought him aid, laboring on into the night with the goat's hair, that he might preach the gospel in the day. I like to think of him taking his lonely way to prison, and at last to death; and then I like to think of the thousands of preachers who are preaching from the words he wrote, and of the whole church as enriched thereby, and helped towards the uplifting of humanity, and the bringing in of the great Kingdom of God.

"But one thing — the things behind forgetting, and to the things before forthreaching — towards the goal I pursue." How did the apostle himself at last reach the personal realization of all the highest things? How I glory in some of the last things Paul wrote! Let us look, not merely at the physical weakness, but look closer, and I pray you, see upon his very body the scars of brutality, the marks of infinite cruelty, the scars in his flesh from the forty stripes save one, the indentations in the flesh of the brutal stones hurled against him. And now listen, "Henceforth let no man trouble me" — splendid independence? Any one might think he had been made a bishop, or called to another church. What is it, Paul? What makes you so independent? "I bear branded on my body the marks, the stigmata, of Jesus." He might have rolled back the robe, and said, See here the stone cut deep, or, See there the prints of Jesus, the stigmata of Christ in the seams left by the cruel whip. The one thing is given you, Paul, that you passionately longed for, suffering with Christ, and through that you have passed into the realization of the crowning and victory of Christ. And when he is coming to the end, he has no confession of failure in the ministry to make. There is no mourning, no sighing. He does not say, It has been a poor business. No, no. "I have fought the good fight, I have finished the course, I have kept the faith." He could never have sung some hymns we sing. He could never have sung that hymn about "Safe home, safe home in port." That, however, was not Paul's idea of getting into port.

> Safe home, safe home in port,
> And only not a wreck,
> Rent cordage, shattered deck.

Men and women ought to be ashamed to sing it. Paul did not drift into port with rent cordage, and tattered sails, and only not a wreck. He went out to sea with every inch of canvas stretched to catch the breeze.

If you and I would come at last to the margin, and find the infinite sea beyond filled with light and glory, and would know the victory of a full-sailed life, we must get back and say, "One thing." Oh, for this vision and virtue, and oh, for the victory! It is the man of one thing that becomes the man of many things, and finally becomes the man of one thing in all-inclusive glory.

Will you look once again through those pillars of Hercules? What see you? *Plus Ultra?* More beyond? Life beyond you. Strenuous life as you believe and hope. Successful life, as we desire and pray for you. But have you fixed your pillars there? Have you written just over the success, *Ne Plus Ultra?* Oh, I beseech you, look once again. Look further! I declare to you that through the pillars where you have now put them, there is still *Plus Ultra;* the supernal vocation of God in Christ Jesus, the life for which all life is but a school and a preparation. This is the school time, and we are all at school still. But presently there is commencement, passing out into the eternal. Get that vision and obey it, and these nearer things toward which you look today, life, life strenuous, life successful, these nearer things will not perish, they will not be spoiled, but they will be made to contribute to the great finality, and so find their own fulfilling.

> Come, let us quickly fling ourselves before Him,
> Cast at His feet the burthen of our care.
>
> Flash from our eyes the glow of our thanksgiving,
> Glad and regretful, confident and calm,

Then thro' all life and what is after living
  Thrill to the tireless music of a psalm.

Yet, thro' life, death, thro' sorrow and thro' sinning
  He shall suffice me, for He hath sufficed:
Christ is the end, for Christ was the beginning,
  Christ the beginning, for the end is Christ.

FOUNDATIONS

If the foundations be destroyed, What can the righteous do?
—Psalm 11:3

Nᴏᴛʜɪɴɢ! Iꜰ the foundations be destroyed, the righteous are hopeless and helpless. But are the foundations in danger?

This psalm is attributed to David. Opinions differ among those who hold this view, as to the circumstances under which it was written. Some refer it to the days of Saul's persecution, and some to those sadder and darker days of Absalom's rebellion.

And again, it is not easy definitely to decide whether the psalm is the record of a conflict between a man of faith, and those who were actuated by fear; or the record of an inward struggle between faith and fear.

Let us say at once that none of these things matters. Whether David wrote the psalm or not is of little moment. The peculiar and local circumstances under which it was written are of no importance in our study. Whether the advice of fear and the affirmation of faith, were those of two men in controversy, or those of two voices within the soul, is practically of no consequence.

That which is of interest and value is that the psalm reveals a conflict between faith and fear in an hour of difficulty and of danger, which conflict resulted in the victory of faith.

In order that this may be clearly before the mind, let us take time to examine the whole psalm.

Such examination will reveal the fact that the words selected as the basis of our meditation are those of fear, and not those of faith. They constitute part of the advice to the man of faith, or of the voice of fear within his own soul.

The psalm opens with a great affirmation of confidence,

In Jehovah put I my trust.

In immediate connection the question is asked,

How say ye to my soul?

and there follows the repetition of the thing which had been spoken, the advice given, against which faith was making its protest.

Let us then look at that advice, separated from the language of protesting faith;

Flee as a bird to your mountain;
For, lo, the wicked bend their bow,
 the string,
That they may shoot in darkness at
 the upright in heart.
If the foundations be destroyed,
What can the righteous do?

In these words we have advice given to this man, either by friends of his, or by the fears of his own heart, the tremblings of his own spirit.

Against that advice faith protested as it enquired.

How say ye to my soul?

and the ground of the protest is revealed in the affirmations of the rest of the psalm.

In Jehovah put I my trust:
 *   *   *   *
Jehovah is in his holy temple,
Jehovah, his throne is in heaven;
His eyes behold, his eyelids try, the
 children of men.
Jehovah trieth the righteous:

> But the wicked and him that loveth
>   violence his soul hateth.
> Upon the wicked he shall rain snares;
> Fire and brimstone and burning wind
>   shall be the portion of their cup.
> For Jehovah is righteous; he loveth
>   righteousness:
> The upright shall behold his face.

Comprehensively then it may be said that we have in this psalm, the advice of fear and the answer of faith, in the midst of circumstances of grave and imminent peril, resulting from malice and treachery. The righteous man is seen in danger from threatened violence on the part of the wicked; and fear, prudent fear, politic fear, utters its advice as it charges him, Flee man, flee as a bird to your mountain; flee away from the place of peril. Your standing is crumbling beneath your feet because the foundations are destroyed.

To such advice faith replies,

> Jehovah is in his holy temple,
> Jehovah, his throne is in heaven;
> His eyes behold, his eyelids try, the
>   children of men;

and therefore flight is unnecessary. Fear says, Flee to the mountain. Faith replies, I cannot flee, I dare not flee, I need not flee.

Let us now examine more particularly this advice of fear and this answer of faith.

THE ADVICE OF FEAR

The final word of the advice is that of the text.

> If the foundations be destroyed,
> What can the righteous do?

The whole argument of fear is based upon the supposition that the foundations are destroyed, and in the statement immediately preceding this enquiry, the reasons for believing that they are destroyed are given.

The first is that the wicked are in opposition. The picture drawn is a very graphic one. It is that of determined and imminent violence. The bow is already bent, "the wicked bend their bow"; the arrow is fixed upon the string, ready to take its flight, "they make ready their arrow upon the string"; and the target of the arrow is the righteous man, against whom the wicked have set themselves in array.

Moreover this opposition of the wicked as seen in the picture, is not fair and above board; it is not opposition in the open;

> That they may shoot in darkness at
> the upright in heart.

There, hiding in ambush, in the darkness, stealthily, is the enemy, with the bow bent, and the arrow ready to take its swift flight for the heart of the righteous man; and because of that, the advice is given, Flee, flee as a bird to your mountain.

That view of the nature of the peril constitutes the conviction that the foundations are destroyed. Fear declares: This is not an even conflict; murder is not warfare; your case is hopeless because your enemy will not come out into the light. This attitude and threatened activity is the outcome of the mastery of passion. Law no longer reigns. If the fight were on a fair field and without favor, you might stay and contend, but those in opposition are adopting the methods of subtlety and deceit. What can the righteous do under such circumstances? If the foundations be destroyed the righteous can do nothing.

The inference of the question is perfectly fair and absolutely correct; if the foundations be destroyed, the righteous will be destroyed, if he remain where he is. Therefore the appeal of fear is logical; it is better that the righteous man should fly. Let him fly as a bird, let him fly and seek his own personal safety; let him give up his attempt to stand for righteousness and to establish it. Let him away to the mountains and secure, at least his own safety. If the foundations are gone, building is impossible. Let the man in danger see to himself.

Before listening to the answer of faith, let us enquire wherein the mistake of the advice of fear consists. It is in the fact that the outlook of the one giving the advice, is limited; and therefore the advice is false. Fear never sees the whole of the facts. Fear is always nearsighted. The supposition of this advice is the result of a mistaken conception of what foundations really are. Supposing for the moment that this was actually the advice of a friend of David, given to him in some hour of imminent danger, then it is evident that he imagined that the fairness of enemies constituted a foundation, and that if foes had ceased to be fair, the foundations were failing. The advice was born of the conception that circumstances are foundations. That is entirely false. Circumstances are only scaffolding. This advice was given by one who looked at a day, as though in it the whole of a life could be seen; at that which is immediate, as though by observation of it, there could be perfect understanding of all the forces bearing upon that life. As he looked, the near things were those of enmity and hostility. The supreme vision was that of a subtle foe who had lost a sense of fairness, and who lurked in the darkness with the bow bent, and the arrow upon it, ready to speed on its flight for the destruction of the righteous man. To one with that outlook upon life, the foundations were indeed destroyed.

Yet though all that was wrong, I am constrained to say that I should not have known it was wrong, had it not been for the answer of the man of faith. It was a subtle word, this word of fear spoken to David, either by a friend, or by the trembling of his own nature. It was a plausible word, having in it all the elements of logic, and policy, and wisdom. Who shall gainsay it? No man can gainsay that advice unless he have the vision of the man who answered. Blot out for me what remains of this brief psalm; deny the affirmations which follow, and I have no course open other than that of flight as a bird to the mountains. Apart from these affirmations I shall abandon all hope and all endeavor; for the forces massed against right are mighty, and the most terrible fact in the fight for righteousness is that the forces against it do not come into the open. They lurk in dark and hidden places, and shoot privily, until it does seem as though the very foundations were gone.

THE ANSWER OF FAITH

The answer of faith is first that of a general affirmation.

In Jehovah put I my trust,

followed by a careful declaration of the reasons for that trust.

The first of these reasons is thus stated,

Jehovah is in his holy temple,
Jehovah, his throne is in heaven.

Other reasons follow, at which we shall presently look, and perhaps they seem to touch us more nearly. They seem to help us a little more immediately, but as this was the first in the thought of the psalmist, it is for evermore the first in the actual facts of life.

I am not at all sure in my own mind, let me at once admit, as to the exact and final sense in which two great words are being much used in present day discussions. I refer to the words "immanence" and "transcendence"; the immanence of God, and the transcendence of God. While I have some idea of the simple meaning of the two words, I am afraid that idea does not help me to understand the use of terms to which I have referred. What some men mean I confess I do not know, and I may parenthetically remark that I am not perfectly sure that they know what they mean. But let that pass, and taking the simple suggestions of the word, I affirm that the first fact creating faith in the heart of this man was not that of the immanence of God, but that of His transcendence.

Not that God is close at hand, intimately associated with all the facts and forces in the midst of which we live — without that fact we cannot live, and to a consideration of it we come presently — but that God is higher than the earth, away from it, even while close to it. He is in His temple. His throne is in heaven, and as another psalm declares,

> His Kingdom ruleth over all.

That is the first fact upon which faith fastens; that He is in His temple, that His throne has never yet been shaken or rendered vacant, in spite of all attempts made against it; which attempts have inevitably resulted in failure.

> Jehovah is in his holy temple

above the conflict in the place of serene and impartial judgment. If I lose that conviction — I speak for myself — if I lose that sense of God, nothing will make me master of fear. If He be none other than near; if He be merely one among many forces; or if He be merely the sum total of these forces which are contradictory and in conflict; then I am not sure of what the issue may be, of which element will at last be victorious.

This then is the first vision; Jehovah is in His temple, His throne is in the heaven. He is above the strife, and beyond it. It cannot ultimately triumph over Him, or shake His throne. He abides on the throne of His government in the quiet serenity of His eternity. That is the first fact upon which faith fastens.

But that is not the final fact. He is not enthroned apart, in ignorance, or in indifference;

> His eyes behold, His eyelids try, the
> children of men.

The figurative language of the term is almost startling, as so often is the case in these Old Testament Scriptures where the picture presented by a word is so graphic that we are almost afraid to translate literally, and to follow the thought suggested.

The statement of faith here is that God is not merely on the throne; He is watching, He is observing; and the figure suggested by the two words, is that of One bending over, and minutely and earnestly contemplating all that is passing before His eyes. He sees the man in the dark with the bow bent, and the arrow ready to fly. He sees the man who is the intended target of that arrow; and I repeat, the words of the psalmist are startling, as they reveal the intensity of the observation of Jehovah.

Just as in the prophecy of Malachi, we have that wonderful word spoken of the attitude of God toward His people as He listened to them, "The Lord hearkened and heard"; so here the attitude is revealed by the declaration, "His eyes behold, his eyelids try." In the description of the listening of God, "The Lord hearkened and heard," we have not the same word twice repeated; two ideas are suggested. The Hebrew word translated "hearkened" literally means "pricked his ears." The figure is that of a horse, pricking his ears, listening to every tone of its master's voice. The Hebrew word translated "heard" means to bend over, in order not to miss a single syllable.

So here, the declaration "His eyes behold," conveys the idea of the most intense gaze in order to perfect perception of the fact; while the second declaration "His eyelids try," suggests that fluttering of the eyelids in rapid closing and opening over the eyes, when the purpose is to test, to investigate, to discriminate, to be perfectly sure.

All this is, to use the term of the theologians, anthropomorphic, the speaking of God as one would speak of a man, which is a perfectly correct thing to do; indeed, it is the only way in which it is possible for man to understand God, who is Spirit; and the ultimate vindication of the method is that of the Incarnation.

The thought of the psalmist is that Jehovah, who is in His temple, who is on the throne, is not indifferent. He is watching, and that with the minutest care; so that nothing escapes His observation. All that fear has seen, God has also seen; only fear has not seen God.

But the outlook of the psalmist takes in more than these first facts. Not only is it true that God is in His temple, and that He is enthroned; not only is it true that He is perfectly conscious of all that is going on, watching, considering, observing; it is also true that He is active.

The first fact of His activity is revealed in the declaration, "He trieth the righteous," by which the man of faith declares that the very circumstances of difficulty in which he finds himself are not only known to Jehovah, but are under His control, they are part of God's method.

> How say ye to my soul,
> Flee as a bird to your mountain?

I cannot flee, first because God is in His temple, and is enthroned; secondly because God is watching; but thirdly and supremely because He is trying me by these very circumstances. I dare not flee, I dare not attempt to escape the pressure by which He is trying me. He is active in the midst of the very circumstances that have constrained fear to make its appeal for flight, and that consciousness makes flight impossible. It is that conviction which compels the man of faith to sing,

> O Cross, that liftest up my head,
>   I dare not ask to fly from Thee;
> I lay in dust life's glory dead,
> And from the ground there blossoms red,
>   Life that shall endless be.

And again, God is not only active in the midst of the circumstances that try the righteous, He is active in judgment against the wicked. He will rain snares and fire and brimstone upon the evil.

Thus the man of faith sees Jehovah not merely enthroned, not merely watching, not impassive; but holding the reins, already at work, and ready to interfere at the right moment; actually at work, making use of the strain and stress of the hour, making use of all the forces massed against the man of faith, making use of the very enmity of foes, making use even of the apparent break up of order. Himself, in His being and in His activity, the Ultimate Foundation, when all other foundations seem to be gone; He is making use of all these things for the perfecting of the character of the man who seems to be in peril, and for the bringing of that man into true relationship with Himself. Therefore to all hostility there is the limit of His government. The arrow may be upon the string, the bow may be bent to its utmost, the enemy may now purpose to allow it to wing its way to the heart of the righteous man; but it can never strike unless God permit; and upon the evil who attempt by subtlety to destroy the righteous, He will rain snares and brimstone and a burning wind.

The Lord is in His temple, in the place of calm and unruffled serenity. From that height He is watching, so that He knows the way I take, its sorrows, its difficulties, its perils; so that He sees the foes and the forces that are massed against me; and He is not only thus enthroned and observant, He is active. By these very things He is trying me, and perfecting that which concerneth me, and at last He will overcome all my foes.

Such was the outlook of faith, and for one having such an outlook the answer was reasonable, logical,

> How say ye to my soul,
> Flee as a bird to your mountain?

To a man who has this vision of God, as high and lifted up, enthroned in the eternal quiet of the temple; yet watching, so that no detail escapes His knowledge; and perpetually active in the midst of all the forces in which that man lives, flight is impossible, flight is unnecessary, flight would be sinful. If the foundations are destroyed, what can the righteous do? But the foundations are not destroyed, therefore,

> How say ye to my soul,
> Flee as a bird to your mountain?

Mark well the two logics of the psalm; the logic of human wisdom and prudence, which lacks the larger vision of God; and the logic of human wisdom and prudence which is the result of the vision of God. The former has but one word of advice to men in places and hours of peril; Flee, flee! In face of danger, grave, imminent, and subtle; in the day when the forces in opposition seem to be more and mightier than we are able to contend with; then we are constrained to declare that the foundations are gone, and it were wiser to abandon the struggle and take refuge in flight. All this is preeminently logical, if our vision be only that of circumstances.

But there are men and women who have climbed far higher than that. As to circumstances they are budgeted, storm-tossed, and in peril; and with best intention, friends observing only these things of difficulty, urge them to fly, and the prudent fears of their own soul make the same appeal. Yet because of the larger vision, their answer to all the advice of fear is that of the psalmist;

> How say ye to my soul, Flee?

I cannot flee, I dare not flee, I need not flee; for Jehovah is in His temple, He is watching, He is active.

We all have our days of darkness, when the outlook seems almost hopeless, when the foundations seem as though they were destroyed, in personal life, in home life, in national life; and in such days the temptation that urges flight is sure to come.

Perhaps some of our best friends; best that is, in the sense of their true human love and affection. but who lack the vision of eternity, the sense of the spiritual, will say to us, Give up the struggle, Flee as a bird to your mountain; all this high ideal of yours is fanatical! If the foundations be destroyed, what shall the righteous do? You have no fair chance. If indeed, you were called upon to fight on a fair field, and without favor, we would advise you to continue the conflict, but this is not so. Your enemies are hidden, they are stealthy, they are without principle. Give up the struggle. Why do you still strive for a national ideal of righteousness? Why not give it up? That is the language of fear, and it is the language of unbelief. The hour in which we live is in many senses one of grave and peculiar peril, and reverently, I say, God knows it would be easier to run away, while we look at the things seen. We feel sometimes as though it were of the essence of rest to abandon all toil. We have tried and fought and striven for the coming of the Kingdom of God in London, and there are hours in which we are inclined to say nothing has been done. Is it all worth while? The foundations are destroyed.

But they are not! The attitudes of the foe do not constitute foundations. Circumstances are not foundations. Let us seek the right view-point as we start again, and if we have that view-point, then the psalmist's affirmation will be ours;

> The Lord is in his holy temple,
> The Lord, his throne is in heaven.
> His eyes behold, his eyelids try, the
> children of men.

That central fact of His activity is one upon which we need to fasten our faith in these days. We may change the wording but not the fact.

> He trieth the righteous.

That is a statement needing no change.

If we will express the thought of His judgment in the terms of the hour, we may declare that He will end the iniquity, however strong it be, however subtle its method, however devilish its insidiousness, however it lurk in hidden places. He will drag it into the light, and smite it by the breath of His fiery wrath to ultimate death. That is our confidence.

If that be our view-point then we shall set our faces to the future full of hope and full of courage. We cannot flee, we cannot seek personal safety in flight, because it is unnecessary. Our safety does not consist in escape to the mountains, but in our abiding in our calling with God. That three-fold vision of Jehovah will rob temptations of their power, will make flight impossible, because it will give us to see that flight would be sinful,

> For right is right, since God is God;
> And right the day must win;
> To doubt would be disloyalty,
> To falter would be sin.

Therefore, exactly where we are, though it be in the place of peril, with enemies lurking in the darkness, we will abide.

> In Jehovah put I my trust.
> How say ye to my soul,
> Flee as a bird to your mountain?

TO DIE IS GAIN

To die is gain. — Philippians 1:21

THIS IS THE Christian attitude toward death. Other men than Christians have sometimes made use of the words, but never in such setting as this. Men overwhelmed with sorrow, driven to despair by the difficulties of life, and passionately desiring to escape, have been known to declare that death would be a release, and so gain. But whenever any other than a Christian man speaks of death as gain, it is simply because he desires to escape from the burdens he knows, and is willing through such escape to venture the burdens he knows not. But the setting of my text is different. Here is a man to whom life is a delight, a rapture, to whom the service of life is something to be pre-eminently desired, to whom "to live is Christ," to whom therefore all life has become a song, upon whose horizon all the colors of the rainbow mingle into perfect light, who yet writes the words, "to die is gain," and a little further on repeats the sentiment in slightly altered words, "to depart . . . is very far better."

The dread of death is universal. It is to be found stamped upon the pages of our literature. It is an ever-present conscious-ness in human hearts. It was Bacon who said: "Men fear death, as children fear to go in the dark; and as that natural fear in children is increased with tales, so is the other."

It was Byron who wrote:

> Oh, God! it is a fearful thing
> To see the human soul take wing
> In any shape, in any mood!

It was Shakespeare who declared:

> Death is a fearful thing.
> The weariest and most loathed worldly life
> That age, ache, penury and imprisonment
> Can lay on nature, is a paradise
> To what we fear of death.

It was Young who sang:

> The vale of death! that hush'd Cimmerian vale,
> Where Darkness, brooding o'er unfinished fates,
> With raven wing incumbent, waits the day
> (Dread Day!) that interdicts all future change.

These are but illustrations of the truth that the dread of death is everywhere, and yet we open our Bible and read the writing of a man who says, "to die is gain," "to depart ... is very far better."

In order that we may understand the triumph of such declarations, we propose to consider, first, the Christian view of the fact of death; and secondly, the Christian revelation of the condition of the departed.

"To die," says the apostle. What does he mean? What is the conception of death that occupies the mind of New Testament writers? That is our first question.

I invite you to consider certain words that occur in the New Testament, and their signification as it answers this inquiry. In the account of the transfiguration of our Lord occurs the first word to which I would draw your attention. It is said that there appeared unto Him two men talking with Him, and these were Moses and Elijah, and they spoke with Him "of his decease which he was about to accomplish at Jerusalem." I am inclined to say that there was never a more unfortunate translation than the use of the word "decease" at that point. There is a sense in which it is not wrong, but the word has become so closely associated with popular conceptions concerning death that it is clouded in gloom, and its use here has certainly not aided men in understanding what Christ's outlook upon death was from the Mount of Glory. The word "decease" itself comes to us, as you will remember, from the Latin *decessus,* which means literally "a going out from," and therefore the word is perfectly correct, for Moses and Elijah talked with Jesus upon the Mount of His "going out from." They talked of His exodus, the actual word standing upon the page of the original manuscript being the word *exodou.* Now, while the meaning of exodus and decease are identical, is it not true that the two words do not suggest the same meaning to mind? And yet what Moses and Elijah really talked of with Jesus was not His decease in our abused understanding of the meaning of the word, but simply of His exodus, His going out. Let us keep that in mind for a moment.

Now, if we turn over to Peter's epistle, which is colored with the light and the glory that flashed upon the Holy Mount, we find that Peter writes these words, "after my decease," literally, again, "after my exodus," using in reference to his own death the exact word that had been used concerning the death of Christ on the Holy Mount. There Jesus Himself was transfigured before the disciples; Moses and Elijah stood in the light of the transfigured Christ; the disciples gathered around Him were also in the light of that same transfigured Person; and indeed, all the mountain flamed with the light of the transfiguration glory. Peter came down from the Mount, passed on through the experiences of the after-days — the sad and awful experiences that lay before him — was restored to the joy and fellowship of communion with Christ, and then established his brethren as the Lord instructed him, by writing of these epistles. In writing to the Christians of the dispersion he used the same word of his own death that had been used of Christ's death, "after my exodus."

This word "exodus" only occurs three times in the New Testament, once with reference to the death of Jesus, once with reference to the death of Peter, and once in the letter to the Hebrews, where the reference is to the actual coming out of Israel from Egypt in olden times. The meaning of the word is seen by its use in connection with the liberation from Egyptian bondage of the chosen people of God.

Still one other word to which I would draw your attention. Paul, writing to Timothy, in his second epistle, says, "after my departure." Here the word is not the same, but it has a similar thought, although the figure is slightly different. While the word "exodus" means a going out of, the word "departure" means a losing from. The word "departure" is a nautical word, and it suggests a ship which has been moored to the shore, the rope flung off, the anchor lifted, and the ship moving out of harbor away on to the wide and boundless sea; and thus when the apostle referred to his going, he did not refer to it as a coming into harbor, but as a going out from harbor to the great wide sea. "After my departure."

Now, let us make our deductions. What is an exodus? A going out from slavery into liberty, a going out from limitation into unlimited life, a going out from burdens and bondage into freedom and spaciousness. That is the word which is made use of in connection with the death of Jesus, and which Peter made use of in connection with his own death. It suggests an exodus: going out from slavery into liberty, departure from bondage and limitation, finding the way out into all the freedom of unlimited, unrestrained and unrestricted life.

When Paul speaks of his departure he speaks of it as the loosing of a ship from its moorings and its setting free from the shore, passing out from that which checks and holds it, and prevents the fulfilling of its highest function. On the sea it can fulfil the possibility of its own being, and prove itself worthy by fulfilling the purpose for which it was constructed.

In these two words we have this revelation, therefore, of the Christian thought concerning death: that death is not the end, but the beginning; that when a Christian passes through the valley of the shadow of death he takes his way into the land of perfect light and perfect realization. How largely the church has suffered from misinterpretation of the meaning of death in her hymnology I think it would be difficult for us to say, and yet there have been some of our poets who have caught the true Christian idea of death. You remember Tennyson's "Crossing the Bar," and the figure used therein. It is not the figure of a ship coming into harbor, but the figure of a ship passing out of harbor and finding its life and freedom and liberty on the sea.

> Sunset and evening star,
>   And one clear call for me!
> And may there be no moaning of the bar,
>   When I put out to sea.
>
> But such a tide as moving seems asleep,
>   Too full for sound and foam,
> When that which drew from out the boundless deep
>   Turns again home.
>
> Twilight and evening bell,
>   And after that the dark!
> And may there be no sadness of farewell
>   When I embark.
>
> For tho' from out our bourne of Time and Place
>   The flood may bear me far,
> I hope to see my Pilot face to face
>   When I have crossed the bar.

Carefully notice the idea. Let me put it into contrast for a moment with another verse:

> Safe home, safe home in port!
>   Rent cordage, shattered deck;

> Torn sails, provision short,
>   And only not a wreck;
> But oh, the joy upon the shore
> To tell our voyage perils o'er!

That is part of a popular hymn, and it is absolutely false. Tennyson's "Crossing the Bar" many people would hardly dare to sing as a hymn, and yet it is absolutely Scriptural and spiritual. That picture of death as the coming into port of a poor dismasted, dismantled, half-ruined wreck is utterly false to the whole New Testament conception of death; but this of a ship loosed from its moorings, crossing the bar, putting out to sea, and meeting the Pilot face to face, that is indeed the New Testament picture of death.

In the "Passing of Arthur," Tennyson is true to the same figure:

> So said he, and the barge with oar and sail
> Moved from the brink, like some full-breasted swan
> That, fluting a wild carol ere her heath,
> Ruffles her pure, cold plume, and takes the flood
> With swarthy webs.

That is the true picture of death.

Or, most exquisite of all, two little verses from the pen of Bret Harte perfectly tell the story of what death really is.

> As I stand by the cross on the lone mountain's crest,
>   Looking over the ultimate sea,
> In the gloom of the mountain a ship lies at rest.
>   And one sails away from the lea:
> One spreads its white wings on a far-reaching track.
>   With pennant and sheet flowing free:
> One hides in the shadow with sails laid aback,
>   The ship that is waiting for me!
>
> But lo, in the distance the clouds break away!
>   The Gate's glowing portals I see;
> And I hear from the outgoing ship in the bay
>   The song of the sailors in glee;
> So I think of the luminous footprints that bore
>   The comfort o'er dark Galilee,

> And wait for the signal to go to the shore,
> To the ship that is waiting for me.

"After my going out, after my departure!" The supeme lesson of the words to which I have drawn your attention is that, in the Christian view, death is the portal of life, the loosing of the ship form its moorings. The ship, which when moored to the shore has yet seemed to be a veritable thing of life as waves gently beating in against her have lifted her, and she has seemed to sigh and sob and fret for the ocean itself, presently loosed from her moorings, passes out from harbor and on to the bosom of the great and mighty deep. Then the meaning of her maker is known and her true function is fulfilled. A ship is for the sea rather than for the port. That is the picture represented in Paul's word "departure." It is as though he had said: I am here, a ship, made for the ocean, but bound to the shore; a ship made for the infinite reaches of the boundless main, and yet fastened to the limitations of the present life. "After my departure," presently the anchor will be lifted, presently the rope will be flung off, presently I shall feel the thrill and the force of the endless life wrapping me round about and bearing me on its bosom. "To depart" — and the word is the same in its root meaning — "and be with Christ," to be free from the limitations of the present, to have done with the things that confine and limit and localize and hinder, to be out upon the spacious and the boundless and the infinite main. That is always, under one figure of speech or other, the Christian outlook upon death.

We have too often spoken as though death were the coming into harbor, as though death meant rest, as though death meant sleep. These things are all true, but they are not the perfection of the truth; they are not the finality of truth. Coming into harbor, yes. But for what? To pass through it into the larger sea that stretches beyond. Rest surely, yes, but not freedom from service and from work, but infinite capacity for working without weariness. Sleep, yes, surely, the quiet falling on sleep to wake in the presence of the living Lord who has ever been nearer than we knew, and whom as we wake we see and know and find to be our own. The Christian view of death, therefore, I repeat, is that of going out into the larger life, and not coming into anything that is narrower than that which has been our experience here and now.

But now, secondly, what is the Christian revelation of the condition of the departed? Accepting this view of death, we come down to the shore as the loved one goes, and watch the loosing of the tackle, the casting off of the ropes, the taking in of the anchor, and we see the ship move out to sea. We stand, as Bret Harte suggests, upon the lone mountain crest, looking over the ultimate sea, and hear the song of the sailors in glee; but standing on that margin we strain our eyes peering into the distances, and the very certainties of our faith appeal to our hearts, and create a longing desire for yet fuller, larger knowledge concerning those who have passed to that great ultimate sea.

There are things we know. We know that the loved ones abide, for the world is that which passeth away, and its lusts are they that perish, but those who do the will of God abide for ever. We know that their condition is that of perfectly conscious blessedness, for there can be no more effective words on this subject than the simple statement of Holy Scripture, "absent from the body, . . . at home with the Lord."

And yet there are so many other questions rising. How can it be gain to die? If indeed it is gain to die, what constitutes the gain, wherein lies the element of gain to our loved ones? They left work here that seemed so important; they left ministries here in which we seem as though we could not do without them; they left great aching voids behind that it seems as though their presence must be necessary to fill. What gain can it be to those who have gone? We ask our question, and let us ever remember that here, as in all cases, "the secret things belong unto Jehovah our God; but the things that are revealed belong unto us and to our children for ever, that we may do all the words of this law." We have no desire to know the hidden things, but we do desire to know intelligently the revealed things. And now in answer to this second question. What is the condition of the departed, the condition which makes it possible for a man to say, "To die is gain," which makes it better to depart, far better to depart? I want to suggest to you four thoughts based upon the distinct declarations of Scripture.

First, the Scripture teaches us that to those who have put out to sea there has come unclouded vision; secondly, that there has come to them perfect correspondence to the infinite Lord and Master; thirdly, that there has come to them full knowledge — that after which they have been seeking comes to them like break of day, as crossing the bar, they see the Pilot face to face; and lastly, and supremely, the culminating fact, for which all those to which I have made reference are but preparatory, they have entered upon perfect and unceasing service, for which all the service of earth was but the training and the preparation. These are the great revealed facts. Minor details are denied us. Many things still we want to know, but we must wait until we also put out to the great ultimate sea, and know fully; but these things are told us.

"For now we see in a mirror, darkly; but then face to face." "We shall see him even as he is." The twofold testimony of Paul and John; the testimony of the Spirit through the man of logical mind, and through the man of keen poetical interpretation of deepest truths. I read the first; it is the language of Paul. Paul wanted to see again the vision he had seen, and always seemed to be restless in his absence from his Lord. "We see in a mirror, darkly." How much he saw, and yet by comparison with what to him was the certainty of the glorious vision he said: "It is but in a mirror, darkly; but then face to face." And John, the mystic, said, "We shall see him as he is." Faith having had its perfect work, is to be vindicated, and crowned by sight, and I venture to affirm as the deep conviction of my heart that the first joy of the departed is the vision of the Lord Himself. I do not propose to enter into any argument concerning the localization of Jesus in the glory. That the Man of Nazareth is there, as a Man, is certain; and it is the actual vision of His dear face to which we all look forward.

Bishop Bickersteth, in his poem, "Yesterday, To-day, and For Ever," a poem in which fine imagination is guided by deep spiritual insight, describes the passing of a saint from earth to the presence of the King. An angel is supposed to bring the spirit, freed from the body of humiliation, to an appointed place, and then to withdraw with the words:

> ... alone
> Thou seest Him whom thou has loved unseen:
> That is an incommunicable joy
> In which no other hearts, angels or men,
> Can intervene.

Then follows a description of the coming of the Lord to the waiting one.

> I turn'd to see who call'd me; and lo, One
> Wearing a form of human tenderness
> Approach'd. Human He was, but love divine
> Breathed in His blessed countenance, a love
> Which drew me onwards irresistibly
> Persuasive: whether now He veil'd His beams
> More closely than the hour His brightness shone
> Around the prophet by Ulai's banks,
> And in the solitary Patmos smote
> Prostrate to earth the Apocalyptic seer;
> Or whether the Omnipotent Spirit of God
> Strengthens enfranchised spirits to sustain
> More of His glory. I drew near to Him,
> And He to me. O beatific sight!
> O vision with which nothing can compare!
> The angel ministrant who brought me hither
> Was exquisite in beauty, and my heart
> Clave to his heart: the choristers of light,
> Who sang around our pathway, none who saw

Could choose but love for very loveliness.
But this was diverse from all other sights:
Not living only, it infused new life;
Not beautiful alone, it beautified;
Not only glorious, for it glorified.
For a brief space methought I look'd on Him,
And He on me. O blessed look! how brief
I know not, but eternity itself
Will never from my soul erase the lines
Of that serene transfiguring aspect.

A quotation full of beauty, very poor by comparison with the realities it attempts to describe, I doubt not, and yet the best I know apart from inspiration as suggesting something of the meaning of the words, "then face to face." Faith having had its perfect work, is vindicated and crowned by sight, for the loved ones that have passed before us have looked into the face of the crowned and enthroned Son of God.

And yet again, more than that, perfect correspondence to the One upon whom they have looked. What simpler phrase is there in all the New Testament, and what more sublime than this, "We shall be like him"? At last, when those who put out to the ultimate sea look into His face, that which was potential in regeneration becomes realized in glorification, the whole spiritual character harmonizing at last with that of the Lord. You have seen some master musician holding in his hand an instrument, tuning it, and you have heard the discords, and if you have listened with an ear acute you have found that as his hand was upon the chord in the process of tuning, gradually the discord melted away.

As, yes, this is all tuning and tension now, but presently when we see Him He will touch us again as never before, and we shall find that the perfect instrument that He has created and tuned will respond to His thought, and the perfect harmony of life will be reached when all within us answers without discord all that is within Him! He is giving us to-day the chord of the dominant, and He is bidding us find the harmonies. Ah, me!

What discord often! Oh, this training, and this tuning, and this tension! Presently the whole will be over, and when the loved ones see Him they find at last that the final work is done in that moment when they stand before Him and are like Him; all the perfections of His great person theirs, not in measure, but in kind; not in quantity, but in quality. Our loved ones who have passed before have seen Him actually, and have found themselves in spirit and in character in perfect harmony with Him.

And yet again, full knowledge. "Now, I know in part," says the restless spirit of the mighty apostle, "but then shall I know fully, even as also I am fully known." Then there will be explanation of the problems; the perpetually recurring mysteries that have demanded repeated acts of faith will find their answer in the dawning light of the Master's presence. Oh, the problems that were solved when the loved one went on! First, the vision; secondly, the consciousness of correspondence; and then, the sense of the solution of all problems. I do not say that at the first and in a moment they who see the Lord have revealed to their intelligence the final meaning of the fact, but they know in His presence as they are known of Him, and they know that in Him there is solution for all mysteries; and the heart is hushed into the infinite rest of a perfect confidence in the presence of the One seen for the first time.

And yet, beloved, these things to my heart are all preliminary, preparatory, and the greatest truth is that "they serve him day and night in his temple." Now, what dare I say to you about that? How much one can say about it! I never sit down in the presence of that great declaration without feeling my imagination, almost in spite of my attempt to curb it, take wings and fly away.

"They serve him day and night in his temple." What is the nature of the service? I do not know. We are not told. We can only argue something of it from our knowledge of Him into whose presence the loved ones have passed. May I not venture to say at least this much: that being nearer to the Lord and understanding Him more perfectly, they will enter more fully into all the things that are of interest to Him? Concerning the loved ones who have passed before us into closer fellowship with Christ, who have departed to be with Christ in a sense in which we never can be with Him here and now, am I not perfectly safe in supposing that the enterprise of His heart has become, in a measure never before possible, the enterprise of their hearts; that the thing upon which His will is set is that upon which their wills are set; that the thing that He supremely desires is the thing which they supremely desire? Am I not safe in saying that as the risen, glorified Lord is still full of compassion for lost men, so are the loved ones gone before? And so I violate any true canon of interpretation if I venture to say to you that in some way, in some way that I cannot understand, those loved ones who have passed on into the larger life have found a larger sphere of service for the blessing of men, and for the salvation of those upon whom the heart of Christ is set?

You tell me this is speculative; you tell me that to say this is to arouse all kinds of difficulties and questions. I know it, and yet I do not hesitate to say it. You ask me if I can imagine how those loved ones are still serving with Christ in those enterprises. I can imagine one way in which they still may serve. I can believe that they still pray; and I beseech you to draw very clear distinction between what I am saying and anything like the doctrine of the intercession of saints which includes the idea of meritorious efficacy. To imagine that our loved ones gone intercede for us, and by their intercession create merit which counts in the economy of grace, is utterly unwarranted by and indeed contrary to, Scripture; but I cannot, I do not imagine the possibility of a mother who prayed for her boy to the end of life's pilgrimage, passing into the presence of Jesus and becoming indifferent. I must believe that while the limit of that boy's probation lasts, that mother will still pray for him in heaven, and I can imagine — and call all this imagination, and forget it, if you so desire — that the intercessions begun and unanswered here will be continued there. Of course, limits will still be set to such intercession. If those prayed for, in their folly and in their rebellion pass over God's drawn line of limitation, then the prayer will cease, but never until then. I cannot help believing that the loved ones passed away pray still in closer fellowship and in more real communion than ever before, not because of any selfish love that is in their heart for those left behind, but because in closer comradeship with Christ, His love for them crowns, glorifies, fulfils their love for such, and leads them into new lines of perpetual intercession.

Whether they have any other part I know not. Whether they are ever sent upon messages of mercy to the earth I know not. It is certainly strange and interesting how there seems to be an intermixture sometimes in Bible language between the thought of angel service and the thought of the service of men. Angels come, we are told, and yet sometimes when we expect to read that angels come, we read that they are men. I go back to the ascension mount, and I see the little group of men gazing up into heaven, and how often we have been told that two angels came to tell them that Jesus was coming as, and again how often have I seen some picture drawn of angels, brightly winged, telling those men that Jesus was coming. But my Bible tells me that "two *men* stood by them in white apparel; who also said, Ye men of Galilee, why stand ye looking into heaven?" And more than once you will find that those who come to earth are spoken of as men. Not that I think men become angels, or angels become men, but I do believe that sometimes the loved ones return on some spiritual embassy for the King.

I read how angel hands hastened Lot out of Sodom, and sometimes when after I have preached and some young boy has come to me and told me that in the midst of the sermon there came to him the memory of his dead and sainted mother, I have wondered whether it was not merely her prayer in heaven, but whether it might not be true that her very hands were put down upon her boy to hasten him from Sodom into safety.

All imagination, do you say? Well, never forget that human imagination is very weak by the side of the infinite truth; and if these lines of suggested possibilities are all incorrect, at least this is sure: that the loved ones passed out to the infinite life have seen the Pilot face to face, and serve Him day and night.

Oh, it must be so! Those radiant flames of fire whose presence we so sadly miss, do not try to make me believe they are doing nothing, resting merely, careless ever. Nay, nay; all that would imply the condition of hell, and not of heaven. With the Christ they feel His love, with the Christ they cooperate in His service, and in closer union with God and Christ than ever realized here, they serve and work with Him always and ever toward the consummation upon which His heart is set, the infinite victory that yet must come.

And, beloved, may I ask you to notice that these things are logical sequences. Notice them again. Those who have passed out from the limitation of life into the illimitable life, first see Him, and seeing Him they are like Him, and being like Him they know as they are known, and knowing they serve as they have never served. I repeat to you now that the most beautiful thought in all this to my heart is that of the service, and it seems to me that I can state all the other things in relation to the service. They see Him and want to serve Him; they are like Him and are able to serve Him; they know Him and are prepared to serve Him. Seeing, and so desiring; being like, and so able; knowing, and so being prepared, they serve Him.

When first you saw Him you wanted to serve Him. When you see Him, the veil having passed from between you and Himself, do you think the vision will have any other effect?

The proportion in which you and I have been made like Him is the proportion in which we have been able to serve Him.

Think you not that when we are like Him actually and altogether our ability for service will be more perfect than it has ever been?

The proportion in which I know my Lord is the proportion in which I am prepared to serve Him. Is it not certain that when I know as I am known I shall be more perfectly prepared to serve?

Oh, yes, gather up all these four things and you have said but one at last. Inspiration for service in vision; equipment for service in correspondence; preparation for service in knowledge: thus the vision and the correspondence and the knowledge all ministering to, and issuing in service.

And so we think of our holy dead, the "loved long since and lost awhile," not as having drifted into harbor with "torn sails and shattered deck," glad to be saved and that alone; but we think of them as having been but a little while ago loosed from their moorings, meeting the Pilot as they crossed the bar, sailing out on to the ultimate and infinite sea, and to-day serving, working, waiting on the King. How as to detail we know not, but the great certainty is in our heart.

As I close let me say there is one other word of Scripture so full of exquisite tenderness that it must find its place in our meditation. The writer of the letter to the Hebrews, having spoken of all those that had passed on, says, "And these all, having had witness borne to them through their faith, received not the promise, God having provided some better thing concerning us, that apart from us they should not be made perfect." Beloved, this reveals the great bond of union between the loved ones gone before and those of us who turn again to the burden and the conflict of this little while. They are not yet made perfect. Perfect is the vision, perfect is the spiritual correspondence, perfect is the knowledge, perfect is the service, and yet they are not yet made perfect. They still are waiting as we are waiting. Waiting for what? Waiting for His second advent, waiting for that body of His glory which will never be theirs until the morning of resurrection, waiting in perfect peace and perfect power for the utter and final perfection that can only come when His heart is satisfied and His work accomplished.

Then you say, Do you mean to tell me that there is any sense in which there is imperfection yonder? Certainly, yes. Christ is not yet perfected, nor will He be until the whole body is completed in which He is to display His glory through the ages, until the final victory of the Cross is won, and all evil things are cast out. Never until then will He be absolutely perfected, and never until then will they and shall we be perfected. Oh, see you not the beauty of it? In a household regulated by love all the members wait at the board for the coming of all. Show me the house perfectly regulated by love, and you will find that the family will sit together, and all will wait for all. So in the Father's house. The final feast is postponed until the last child is gathered in. Let us, then, return to the duties of our day, our little day that moves so swiftly to its close, with our eyes fixed where their eyes are fixed, on the Lord, waiting as they wait, for His coming again, and for the perfecting of the number of His elect, and the establishment of His reign of righteousness. They are waiting while they serve. Let us serve while we wait. Thus union will be established between us by our mutual loyalty to the living Lord who presides over the whole number of His own, whether here or yonder; and as we take our way, let us never sing, or think, or speak of the possibility presently of coming into harbor only not a wreck, but let us abide in the present service, and remember that if He tarry and we also shall go as they went, our going will be what theirs was, the coming down to the shore, to the ship that is waiting for us, and the loosing of it from its moorings, and our passing over the bar to see the Pilot and to find the ultimate sea.

> "Till He come," O let the words
> Linger on the trembling chords:
> Let the little while between

In their golden light be seen;
Let us think how heaven and home
Lie beyond that "Till He come."
When the weary ones we love
Enter on their rest above,
Seems the earth so poor and vast,
All our life-joy overcast!
Hush, be every murmur dumb:
It is only "Till He come."
See, the feast of love is spread,
Drink the wine and break the bread:
Sweet memorials — till the Lord
Call us round His heavenly board;
Some from earth, from glory some,
Severed only "Till He come."

THE SPIRIT OF THE AGE

I

W E WILL consider the condition of the people at the time when Malachi uttered his prophecy. There is a key-word in the book revealing this condition, a word these people used in reply to every message which the prophet delivered to them, showing what their real attitude was. It is the word "Wherein." Let us consider the seven occasions of its use:

1. Malachi 1:2 — "I loved you, saith the Lord. Yet ye say, *Wherein* hast thou loved us?"

2. Malachi 1:6 — "A son honoreth his father, and a servant his master: if then I be a Father, where is mine honor? and if I be a Master, where is my fear? saith the Lord of Hosts unto you, O priests, that despise my name. And ye say, *Wherein* have we despised thy name?"

3. Malachi 1:7 — "Ye offer polluted bread upon mine altar. And ye say, *Wherein* have we polluted thee?"

4. Malachi 2:17 — "Ye have wearied the Lord with your words. Yet ye say, *Wherein* have we wearied him?"

5. Malachi 3:7 — "Return unto me, and I will return unto you, saith the Lord of Hosts. But ye said, *Wherein* shall we return?"

6. Malachi 3:8 — "Will a man rob God? Yet ye have robbed me. But ye say, *Wherein* have we robbed thee?"

7. Malachi 3:13 — "Your words have been stout against me,

saith the Lord. Yet ye say, *Wherein* have we spoken so much against thee?"

You notice in this last instance, the Authorized Version gives the word "What," which is a peculiar accident of translation. It is the same word in the Hebrew, and ought to have been translated "Wherein," as in the other cases.

Thus we have this word, "Wherein," put by the prophet into the mouth of those people seven distinct times, with reference to seven distinct announcements. He comes to them first of all with the declaration: "I have loved you, saith the Lord," and they say, *"Wherein* hast thou loved us?" Then he says, "Ye have despised the Lord," and they say *"Wherein* have we despised him?" And then: "Ye have polluted my altar," and they say, *"Wherein* have we polluted thine altar?" And then: "Ye have wearied me," and they say, *"Wherein* have we wearied thee?" And then: "Return to me," and they say, *"Wherein* shall we return?" And then: "Ye have robbed me," and they say, *"Wherein* have we robbed thee?" And lastly: "Ye have spoken against me," and they say, *"Wherein* have we spoken against thee?"

This word shows us the condition of these people in a lurid light. The temple is rebuilt, the altar is set up, the sacrifices are offered, the feasts and fasts are alike observed, and to these people — with outward form and ritual, perfect to the very last and minutest detail — the prophecy comes, the Divine complaint is made. And they look at the prophet with mingled astonishment and incredulity, and they say, "Wherein? What do you mean? You charge us with having despised God and polluted His altar, with having wearied Him, and with wandering from and refusing to return to Him, and accuse us of robbing and speaking against Him; we don't see that we have done these things, so why should we be subjected to these accusations? You come and say we despise God's word. Look at our sacrifices and offerings! You tell us that we have polluted the altar. We have brought our gifts! You tell us that we have wearied Him. We don't see where or when! We are not conscious of having done anything to displease Him! You tell us to return. We don't see where we are to return from; we don't see where we are to return to! You tell us we have robbed God. We want to know when? You say we have spoken against God. We don't remember having spoken against Him; when was it?"

What is the significance of this word "Wherein?" These people are not in open rebellion against God, nor do they deny His right to offerings, but they are laboring under the delusion, that because they have brought offerings, they have been true to Him all along. Theirs is not the language of a people throwing off a yoke and saying, "We will not be loyal," but of a people established in the temple. It is not the language of a people who say, "Let us cease to sacrifice, and worship; and let us do as we please"; but it is the language of a people who say, "We are sacrificing and worshipping to please God," and yet He says, by the mouth of His servant, "Ye have wearied me: ye have robbed and spoken against me."

They have been most particular and strict in outward observances, but their hearts have been far away from their ceremonials. They have been boasting themselves in their knowledge of truth, responding to that knowledge mechanically, technically; but their hearts, their lives, their characters, the inwardness of their natures, have been a perpetual contradiction in the eye of Heaven, to the will of God; and, when the prophet tells them what God thinks of them, they, with astonishment and impertinence, look into his face and say, "We don't see this at all!" To translate it into the language of the New Testament — "having the form of godliness, they deny the power." They have passed into the fearful condition of imagining that what God asks for is but the letter, and they are failing to understand that the letter is, at best, but an awkward representation of what God is demanding in the spirit.

I say "awkward," simply because the letter never can convey all the spiritual meanings. When a man is willing to obey the letter with spiritual intent, then God has more to say than the letter can contain. These people have come simply to bear a literal yoke. They are the most orthodox people, and yet their whole heart is outside the matter, and the facts of their lives are hidden, alas! from themselves, so subtle and awful is the influence of getting away from direct and close dealing with God. I say these facts are hidden from their own eyes. They are not conscious of it, but God is changed to their conception. The God of their fathers is not their God. The God of spiritual communion with His people, who walked and talked with the patriarchs, is not their God. The god of Israel in the days of Malachi, the god whom they had invented, and were trying to appease and worship, was the god of trivialities, of mechanical observances, the god who asked for a temple with a set number of stones and corners, the altar of such a shape, and so many sacrifices and prayers, without any reference to character. When the prophet came to these people, he came to a people who were feeling thoroughly satisfied with their religious observances, and were prepared to say, "Wherein have we done this, or failed to do that?"

II

Now let us go further to discover the reason of their condition. Chapter 2 begins with these words: "And now, O ye priests, this commandment is for you"; and verse 7 reads: "For the priest's lips should keep knowledge, and they should seek the law at his mouth: for he is the messenger of the Lord of Hosts." That is the Divine conception of the priesthood. The priest should not only have the knowledge, but should keep it, that is, walk in it, be obedient to it, be the embodiment of the knowledge he holds, of which he is the depositary for the time being. The people "should seek the law at his mouth," for he is the messenger of the Lord of Hosts. More, he is to tell them the will of God, and that not simply as one who possesses it as a wonderful theory, but as one who is himself living within the realm thereof.

That is the ideal. What then has the prophet to say to the priests? (2:8): "Ye are departed out of the way; ye have caused many to stumble at the law; ye have corrupted the covenant of Levi, saith the Lord of Hosts." Now all this teaches us, that at the back of the declension of the people is the declension and corruption of the priest; that the people failed to have a right conception of God, because the priest ceased to give them the true conception. The whole company of the people have passed out of the high spiritual realm of past history, because the priest has tampered with – corrupted as the word is here – the very covenant of God.

In reading Nehemiah in connection with Malachi, you will have noticed something to which I shall ask you to refer for a moment. Nehemiah 13:28-29: "And one of the sons of Joiada, the son of Eliashib, the high priest, was son-in-law to Sanballat the Heronite: therefore I chased him from me. Remember them, O my God, because they have defiled the priesthood, and the covenant of the priesthood and of the Levites." There you have an example, a historic statement of this very thing, the case of a priest marrying the daughter of Sanballat the Heronite.

Read the history of Nehemiah and see how much Sanballat was, or was not, in accord with the purpose of God. Sanballat was the embodiment of the spirit that was antagonistic to the Word and Spirit of God. One of the priests of God has married his daughter, and Nehemiah says with that magnificent vehemence which characterized all his splendid work: "I chased him from me." Why did you do it, Nehemiah? Why did you chase him away? "Because he had defiled the priesthood, by defiling the covenant of the priesthood and the Levites." The same word occurs in Malachi: "Ye are departed out of the way; ye have caused many to stumble at the law; ye have corrupted the covenant of Levi, saith the Lord of Hosts." The priesthood, instead of keeping the law, had "departed out of the way." The priests had announced the law, they had read its articles, they had proclaimed it as law, and then had debased it themselves. Corruption had come into the covenant by the way of the priesthood.

What was the priesthood for? The only reason for its existence was that there should be on the human side a guarding of the articles of the covenant of God, and no man who himself corrupts, tampers with, breaks the covenant, can for a single moment, by his teaching, uphold it; and the trouble at the back of the national declension was the declension of the priesthood. The teachers of the people, the messengers of God, had themselves done despite to the law of God, by proclaiming it as fact, and denying it in their own lives.

This then was the spirit of the age. Formalism, ritual, ceremonial — everything so far as mechanical and outward observance — complete. A Divine messenger came voicing the complaint of God, and the people in astonishment and anger, and with marked impertinence, looked into the very face of high heaven and said, "We don't see this thing at all — Wherein?" And all this because God's appointed messengers have themselves, in life, and work, and conversation corrupted the covenant, and have passed into the region of baseness and contempt in the eyes of the people.

III

There is, I fear, an awful sense in which that picture is a picture of the age in which we live. Never was there a day when organizations were more complete, and outward and mechanical forms of service more numerous than they are now, but I am not going to dwell merely upon ritual.

I have made reference to a verse with which you are all familiar — II Timothy 3:1-4: "This know also, that in the last days perilous times shall come. For men shall be lovers of their own selves, covetous, boasters, proud, blasphemers, disobedient to parents, unthankful, unholy. Without natural affection, truce-breakers, false accusers, incontinent, fierce, despisers of those that are good. Traitors, heady, high-minded, lovers of pleasures more than lovers of God." I ask you very solemnly to read that description and apply it to the age in which we live.

Take the next verse, 5, for it is that to which I wish to come: "Having a form of godliness, but denying the power thereof." Will you — bearing that verse in mind — turn to Paul's letter to the Romans (2:20), and very patiently follow the thought? You must go back for a moment to verse 17 in order to catch the meaning of his words: "Thou art called a Jew — an instructor of the foolish, a teacher of babes, which hast the *form* of knowledge and of the truth in the law." I have read that passage in order that we may bring these two words together. In Romans 2:20 and II Timothy 3:5 you have the same word "form." These are the only two occasions where that actual word occurs in the whole of the New Testament. Of course, you get the word "form" translated from other words, but this word is *morphsis,* and it means "formation" rather than "form." It refers to the possibility of a process rather than to a thing accomplished. When Paul said to Timothy, "In these last days perilous times should come, that men would have the form of godliness and yet deny the power" — he marked a danger more subtle than that of ritualism. It means that in the last days men will actually come to possess the truth itself which is the formative power of godliness, and yet will deny the power. A man may have the very formation of godliness, he may hold the truth, he may be the most orthodox man in the whole city, and yet deny the power.

That is one of the dangers of the present day. Take Christendom at large. You have thousands of people who can give you good reasons for belonging to the church, who have some purity in their lives responding to the claims of Jesus Christ, and seem to be not only maintaining the outward forms, but appear also to hold tenaciously to the truth which is the formative power of the church, and yet whose lives are not in correspondence to the truth they hold.

In this sense there is an element of danger in our great conventions. Do not misunderstand me. I am not undervaluing them. I thank God for the blessed work being accomplished through them, but there are men and women who are able to enunciate the whole scheme, not only of regeneration but also of sanctification, and yet in their actual life — when lifted away from the crowd of their fellow Christians, and from the opinion of their fellow men, into the white light of Divine requirement, which alone reveals character — it can be said of them "denying the power."

Tell such men it is not a new extension scheme, not a discussion of this constitution or that, we need, but a red-hot fire purging out the dross, and they say "Wherein? Have we not all these things? Do we not hold the truth? Are we not orthodox? — Wherein?"

What is at the back of all this? As in the old days, so now, there has been a corrupting of the priesthood, there has been a corrupting of the covenant by the teachers, who ought to have led us into the deep things of God.

What is God's covenant? If you read Hebrews 8 in connection with Jeremiah 31, beginning with verse 31 and reading on, you will find that the covenant of God with His people, for this dispensation, is in advance of the old covenant. That was a covenant in which God was married to His people, and they were to be kept by outward laws, words written upon tables of stone, commandments uttered in their hearing, and the marriage relationship was to be maintained between the chosen people and God, in that covenant, by obedience to those laws.

What is the new covenant? The new covenant is, "I will write my law upon your heart and upon your mind," and the relation of people in the new covenant to God is to be the relation of a new birth, of an actual affinity, of a marvellous identification. I am no longer married to God in the sense of maintaining the relation by obedience to an outward rule of life, but in the union of a child of God, born again in His Spirit; with His law, not given to me from the outside, but written on my mind and on my heart.

Is that covenant corrupted, nay, is not Christendom corrupted from end to end? If a man begin to talk about inward cleansing, about the necessity for the fire-blood cleansing of the nature, before men can live in communion with God, how many there are who say at once, "We are talking of things that are impossible." So long as we who teach corrupt the covenant by going back to Judaism, by lowering the high and awful requirement of actual new birth and spiritual affinity, just so long will the people be content with holding a form of truth and denying the power.

There is then an awful application of Malachi's days and the spirit of his age to this age and to these days. There was a lowering of the standard of the Divine requirement by the priest — using that word in the Divine sense of the messenger of God — and the people boasting too often in their correct theory of worship, super-orthodox, were yet, in their inner life, in the depth of their own nature, in the actual fact of what God alone knows, "denying the power."

Let us go alone into His presence, for that is light, and fire, and life, and ceasing to be content with conventional religion let each one for himself and herself, in that awful Presence say, "O God, save me from mere correctness of view, and that curiosity to know, for the sake of knowing only, which has blighted my life, and make me what Thou wouldst have me to be in actual character."

THE PURIFYING HOPE

MANY PERSONS will ask, What is the practical value of this teaching? The answer to that question is found in I John 2:28 to 3:3.

> And now, my little children, abide in him; that, if he shall be manifested, we may have boldness, and not be ashamed before him at his coming. If ye know that he is righteous, ye know that every one also that doeth righteousness is begotten of him. Behold, what manner of love the Father hath bestowed upon us, that we should be called children of God: and such we are. For this cause the world knoweth us not, because it knew him not. Beloved, now are we children of God, and it is not yet made manifest what we shall be. We know that, if he shall be manifested, we shall be like him; for we shall see him even as he is. And every one that hath this hope set on him purifieth himself, even as he is pure.

I fear that the question to which I have used these verses as a reply too often reveals the fact that the one asking has a wrong conception of the nature and value of truth. It is not a commodity to be stored, but a purifying and sanctifying force, bringing men into harmony with the will of God. The man who seeks mere possession of, apart from obedience to, truth, must fail in his quest. When God reveals Himself to man, obedience prepares for the reception of further and deeper revelations. In this connection we call to mind the declaration of our Lord, "The truth shall make you free"; and the words of His great intercessory prayer, "Sanctify them through thy truth: thy word is truth." It is not a point of indifference as to whether any given view be correct or not. It is of the utmost importance that we devoutly, humbly, and yet earnestly, search out the will of God in the truth of God. What, then, is the particular value of the study of Bible teaching concerning things to come? John, who had such clear understanding of the affinity between Jesus and the believer, says that the hope of the church is to be the reason for, and the power of, purity of individual life in its members.

The Greek word translated "hope" in the passage referred to undoubtedly has the same meaning as the Anglo-Saxon *hopa*. The word is often used in a light way which ignores its true meaning. Hope is a confident anticipation of good things to come, with corresponding effort to reach and attain them. It is not a mere consciousness in the mind, that something of value is to take place in the future. It is the setting of life and purpose toward that which the mind has come to understand and appreciate. The return of our Lord Jesus Christ is uniformly regarded by the apostles as the hope of the church, though they may treat of it under varied aspects, such as the reward of workers, the destruction of evil, meeting with loved ones gone before, and the inexpressible delight of the Lord's presence. Let us examine a few of such passages:

1. ... heirs of God, and joint-heirs with Christ; if so be that we suffer with him, that we may be also glorified with him. For I reckon that the sufferings of this present time are not worthy to be compared with the glory which shall be revealed to us-ward. For the earnest expectation of the creation waiteth for the revealing of the sons of God. For the creation was subjected to vanity, not of its own will, but by reason of him who subjected it, in HOPE that the creation itself also shall be delivered from the bondage of corruption into the liberty of the glory of the children of God. For we know that the whole creation groaneth and travaileth in pain together until now. And not only so, but ourselves also, which have the first-fruits of the Spirit, even we ourselves groan within ourselves, waiting for our adop-

tion, to wit, the redemption of our body. For by hope were we saved: but hope that is seen is not hope: for who hopeth for that which he seeth? But if we hope for that which we see not, then do we with patience wait for it (Romans 8:17-25).

Evidently, in the mind of the apostle, the completion of redemption — that is, the redemption of the body — is the hope of the church.

2. For the grace of God hath appeared, bringing salvation to all men, instructing us, to the intent that, denying ungodliness and worldly lusts, we should live soberly and righteously and godly in this present world; looking for the blessed HOPE and appearing of the glory of our great God and Saviour Jesus Christ (Titus 2:11-13).

In this case the apostle links the church's hope with the epiphany of the glory.

3. Having therefore, brethren, boldness to enter into the holy place by the blood of Jesus, by the way which he dedicated for us, a new and living way, through the veil, that is to say, his flesh; and having a great Priest over the house of God; let us draw near with a true heart in fullness of faith, having our hearts sprinkled from an evil conscience, and our body washed with pure water: let us hold fast the confession of our HOPE that it waver not; for he is faithful that promised (Hebrews 10:19-23).

The translation in the Authorized Version, "Let us hold fast the profession of our *faith*," is inexplicable, when the Greek word there used is rendered *hope* in every other New Testament passage. Faith has been mentioned in verse 22; and, in its fullness, we are to draw near into the holy place. It is the confession of our *hope* that we are to hold fast; and the nature of that hope is evident from verses 25 and 35-37:

Not forsaking the assembling of ourselves together, as the custom of some is, but exhorting one another; and so much the more, as ye see the day drawing nigh. . . . Cast not away therefore your boldness, which hath great recompense of reward. For ye have need of patience, that, having done

> the will of God, ye may receive the promise. For yet a very little while, he that cometh shall come, and shall not tarry.

The coming of the Blessed One is the hope which we are to hold fast, as we come to God in fullness of faith.

> 4. Blessed be the God and Father of our Lord Jesus Christ, who according to his great mercy begat us again unto a living HOPE by the resurrection of Jesus Christ from the dead, unto an inheritance incorruptible, and undefiled, and that fadeth not away, reserved in heaven for you, who by the power of God are guarded through faith unto a salvation ready to be revealed in the last time (I Peter 1:3, 5.)

The hope of the church is, in this aspect, a salvation to be revealed in all its fullness when Jesus Christ Himself shall come.

5. Reverting to the verses with which we started, in the words "He that hath this HOPE," the apostle of love refers to the day when we shall see Christ as He is, and be like Him. It is this hope toward which the church looks with confidence and takes her way through days of patient waiting.

An alteration, apparently trivial, and yet of vital importance to a right estimate of this hope, is made in I John 3:3. Instead of *"this hope in him,"* as in the Authorized, we have "this hope set on Him," and the pronoun should have a capital letter, for it refers to Jesus Christ as the revelation of the Father. "Behold what manner of love the Father hath bestowed upon us, that we should be called children of God"; and the argument proceeds, from the Father through the Son, to the point of hope's purifying effect.

Then, this hope "maketh not ashamed." There is no uncertainty about it, and it cannot be hindered. That which has become the church's beacon, casting a ray of glory upon her dark night, is no false light luring to destruction. This hope, being set upon God in His purpose and arrangement, and not upon our individual life, the circumstances of a day, the conditions of a century, or the changing policy of ecclesiasticism, is lifted clear away from the strife of party and from human uncertainty.

As sure as God is, the hidden Man Christ Jesus, the King whom the heavens have received for a season, must come again: and the light and the glory of that promise is the hope of the church.

If it be indeed true that Jesus is coming; and if, in the wisdom of God, the date of His return has been absolutely hidden from man — how should we live as those to whom God has given that coming as the supreme and only hope of our life? The question answers itself.

This is a purifying hope, because it regulates the attitude of the believer's life toward Christ. Through all the passing years we are to wait for Him, expecting that at any moment, above the din and strife of earth, we may hear His call. There is no other *purifying* hope. I take it for granted that no true child of God cherishes the sordid ambitions of worldly men, such as the hope of wealth or of fame. Yet our *hope* may be set upon an opening for ourselves in the mission field or in the service of humanity at home. As long as hope is set upon service, it is not fixed upon Christ, and *He* should hold full and absolute possession of our hearts. Our lives may be so occupied with things good in themselves, that we do not see the King. In the will of God, however, there is but one attitude for the believer — that of the pilgrim, with loins girt and staff in hand, waiting for the break of day, the coming of the King. Do not misunderstand me. If we are truly waiting for Jesus, we shall not be careless of those for whom He died: and we shall not dare disobey His word which bids us preach the gospel to every creature. But, as far as individual life is concerned, the coming One should fill the heart's vision through all the days and moments.

How will this affect our behavior? I would suggest questions rather than attempt to answer them; for your own minds and hearts will be busy on this point. How should I transact my business, knowing that even as I make an entry in my ledger I may be interrupted by the call of my Master? How should I take my recreation when, at any moment, He may summon me from it to His own presence? The purifying effect of such considerations are evident. We are to serve our generation, live in our homes, do our business, and take our recreation, in readiness to leave all at any moment. Some one says, "That will make a very strained sort of life." I think not.

Mr. Wesley was once asked by a lady, "Suppose that you knew you were to die at twelve o'clock to-morrow night, how would you spend the intervening time?" "How, madam?" he replied; "why, just as I intend to spend it now. I should preach this night at Gloucester, and again at five to-morrow morning; after that I should ride to Tewkesbury, preach in the afternoon, and meet the societies in the evening. I should then repair to friend Martin's house, who expects to entertain me, converse and pray with the family as usual, retire to my room at ten o'clock, commend myself to my heavenly Father, lie down to rest, and wake up in glory."[1]

No man lived a more strong and beautiful life than did John Wesley, and his view of death was that whenever it came he would be found at his duty; and the transition from that duty to heaven's service would be a natural one. Instead of death, let the Lord be expected; and the true attitude of life will be that of quiet pursuit of duty and constant readiness to greet Him.

But you say to me, "Would you like Jesus to come and find you playing with your children?" Why not? I know of no occupation that I believe would be more pleasing to the heart of my King! It would be a proof of my belief in the blessedness of His reign, when the children are to have a perfect playtime.

When Jesus went from earth, the clouds at which His disciples gazed were riven, and an angel appeared, saying:

> Why stand ye looking into heaven? This Jesus ... shall so come in like manner as ye beheld him going into heaven!

that is, in the clouds, not merely in a spiritual sense. Thus, at

---

[1] *Anecdotes of the Wesleys.* — Wakerley.

the earliest moment in the "little while," the attitude of star-gazing was rebuked; and His disciples were sent to the discharge of duty, to look for Him from the midst of loyal service. Alas! that some who profess to believe in the coming of the Lord, should give up all the things which they were intended to sanctify. We are to be busy about our appointed task; to influence our day and generation as far as in us lies, by a reproduction in the power of the Spirit of the pure character of Jesus Christ; and all the while to have a listening ear for the Master's call, and the longing to welcome Him when He comes.

This hope also lights up circumstances. Are you entrusted by God with the great responsibility of riches? Expecting the Lord's return, you will use that wealth for Him. Are your days filled with stress of poverty and necessity for careful planning in regard to means? In the light of that promise, even poverty is transfigured. I am not now discussing the great questions of poverty and wealth. I regard poverty as a curse! God never meant any one to be poor, in the sense of that pinching, grinding want, which gives a man heartache and brainache. There is plenty in the world for every man to live in comfort, and all lack is the result of human mismanagement. The light of that coming upon friendship forbids unholy alliances and ennobles sanctified comradeship; and when it falls upon the graves where our sacred dust rests, how beautiful they become! We shall meet in "the morning."

> Some from earth, from glory some:
> Severed only till He come.

The bright rays of this truth shine for me upon some of the most perplexing problems of the Book of God and of the times in which we live. In my New Testament I find the free-will of man and the sovereignty of God both distinctly taught. These things were long a source of perplexity to me. The view which I strongly hold, that Christ is coming for His church, an elect company out of the multitude of the saved, has solved for me a most difficult problem. I believe that Divine election has reference to membership in the church of the Firstborn, not to personal salvation; and I believe, therefore, that there will be great multitudes saved by the finished work of Christ who are not members of that sacred body.

Christ's coming throws light upon other problems in the Book, in current theological thought, and in present-day life. How can we find comfort in missionary enterprise unless we believe in Christ's coming and the more blessed dispensation which lies beyond? Let the societies add to their statistics the facts that within a year the heathen have multiplied in a ratio far exceeding the number of converts made; and that the proportion of Christians to the mass of mankind is smaller today than it was fifty years ago. Where is your comfort, in view of these facts? Along with a vista of missionary work God appears as being beaten out of His own world! We believe that the King is doing work preparatory to His coming. He is gathering out His church, and in a thousand ways making straight His paths by the proclamation of the gospel in all lands, so that when the ancient people of God shall become His messengers to all peoples they will find a readiness to receive the message as the result. In this view we have hope for the nations of the earth and for the ages which lie ahead.

The light of this truth falls also upon the chaos and unrest of our age — arming of nations, mutual distrust, "wars, and rumors of wars." Man is failing in governmental power; and the hope of the world is that Jesus will come to rule within the lines or His own royal policy. Once take firm hold of this great truth of the coming of the King, and it affords a bright outlook along every avenue of life and brings gladness to the weary heart.

Our responsibility is marked in the passage to which I have more than once referred:

> And now, my little children, abide in him; that, if he
> shall be manifested, we may have boldness, and not be
> ashamed before him at his coming (I John 2:28).

The *if* casts no doubt upon His appearing, but is indicative of a coming at any time. An alternative possibility is here suggested as to the attitude of *Christians* at that coming. They may "have boldness" or "be ashamed."

With regard to the first: the word *"boldness"* (in place of confidence, A.V.), by no means conveys the whole force of the original. The idea is that we may have the freedom of speech which comes of the perfect familiarity of friendship. We all know the diffidence and awkwardness which come of the sense of being out of place, paralyze speech. This, I imagine, would be the position of most of us if granted a personal interview with Queen Victoria. Not only should we be at a loss in regard to deportment, but we should wonder what to say, and be anxious as to whether we had said it aright or not. May God help us so to abide in Christ that when He comes we may not feel the awkwardness which arises from the constraint of being strangers to Him, but that we may be able to say — This is our Master, we have known him by faith and now we see Him. We have poured in to His listening ear the tale of our sorrows in the day of mystery and darkness, and now we may talk with Him face to face (see Isa. 25:9).

Mark the other possibility, ". . . and not be ashamed *from* Him at His coming" (the preposition is *apo,* away from). The picture is that of persons so conscious of unreadiness that they dare not face Him. The root meaning of the word *ashamed* is *disgraced,* so that it is allowable to read, "and not be disgraced from him at his coming." This is not addressed to the outside world, but to the believer in Christ. In that verse there is a very clear division which, to my mind, answers the question whether believers may not pass through the great tribulation. Some will be ready to enjoy freedom of access to Christ and familiarity with Him; but the "little children" of God who have been living only in the elements of the world will be disgraced at His appearing.

What are we to do, as Christian men and women, in the light of these two possibilities? I give two passages from the Epistle, as my closing words: "My little children, abide in him"; "Every one that hath this hope set on him purifieth himself." Those who are abiding in Christ here on earth, who purify themselves as He is pure, separated ones cut clean adrift from the ungodliness of the age, loyal of heart to the King in the days of waiting for Him — these are the men and women who will have boldness in the day of His coming.

Who shall draw the line? I do not. It is for each of us to make application of this truth in solitude.

THE CHURCH EVANGELISTIC

Evangelism apart from the church is impossible. Christ was, and is the one Evangelist. He now fulfills His great work of proclaiming the good tidings through His Body, which is the church. In the four Gospels we have a picture of Christ, and at the opening of His second treatise Luke makes use of words which indicate for us the character of the Gospel narrative, and suggest that of the book of the Acts of the Apostles. "The former treatise I made, O Theophilus, concerning all that Jesus began both to do and to teach, until the day in which He was received up." That sentence reveals to us the character of the Gospel story. The "former treatise" is the story of the beginning of the doing and the teaching of Jesus. The latter is therefore by inference the story of the continuity of the doing and teaching of Christ. In the Gospel Jesus is seen — to use His own suggestive word — "straitened" until His baptism should be accomplished. In the book of the Acts of the Apostles the same Jesus is seen no longer straightened, for the passion-baptism is accomplished, and He risen, ascended, enthroned, has come into new relationship with men by the Holy Spirit, to continue His work through the church by the Spirit. Consequently the evangel proclaimed by Christ in measure during His life, is proclaimed by Christ in fullness through the church by the Holy Spirit in this age.

Evangelism apart from the church is apart from Christ, and is therefore no evangelism. There can be no evangelism save that of Jesus Christ, and that can only be spoken by Christ Himself through His people by the Holy Spirit. Anything calling itself evangelism which is not the outcome of that new life of Christ, realized in the soul of men, and spoken through men by Christ, is not evangelism.

Unattached and unauthorized evangelism, even by individual members of the church of Christ, is to say the least, unwise, and not the most fruitful of permanent results. I do not desire to criticize unkindly any movement that acts independently of the churches, although I do not hesitate to say that I have grave suspicion of everything that boasts that it is undenominational. I have a very great love for everything that is inter-denominational, which is quite another matter. But all unattached, free-lance work, unauthorized and ungoverned by the church, is not the best work possible, and tends to disorder and confusion. We must hold to the very highest doctrine of the church, or our evangelism will be weak and one-sided. Believing therefore that the relation between the church and evangelistic work is all important, we will carefully consider the church as to its creation, its nature, and its purpose.

The New Testament deals with the church in two ways, as catholic and as local; the whole church of the Living God, and a church in any given locality. Sometimes I am asked what church I belong to. When I reply, I am a catholic churchman, I have seen people look surprised. Yet that is exactly what I am. Catholic means universal. The catholic church is the whole church. Such a phrase as "Roman Catholic" constitutes an absurd contradiction of terms. If catholic, then not Roman. If Roman only, then by no means catholic. That is equally true of the term "Anglican Catholic."

The New Testament deals with the whole church, but it also deals with the local church. The word church is used sometimes of the whole church of God, and sometimes of a church in a given locality, as in Ephesus, in Corinth, in Thessalonica, in Philippi.

So far as the records reveal, the Lord only twice in the course of His public ministry referred to the church. He used the word church once in its catholic sense, and once in its local sense, so that the general New Testament uses of the word harmonize with that of Christ.

The first occasion was when Peter had made the supreme confession of the Messiahship of Jesus, "Thou art the Christ." At that parting of the ways the first half of our Lord's work was accomplished. He had taught a little group of men, the nucleus of His Kingdom, that He was the Christ, the Anointed, the Messiah of God. And then He immediately commenced to teach them a new thing, to bring down into view of the pathway through which the Messiah should accomplish the purpose of God. He began to talk to them of the Cross, but before mentioning the Cross He said to Peter, "Thou art Peter, and upon this rock I will build my church; and the gates of Hades shall not prevail against it." That is a perfect, final, and all-inclusive declaration concerning the church. First, "Upon this rock I will build my church." Secondly, "the gates of Hades shall not prevail against it," not one thing repeated, but two distinct facts about the church. I think we have too often read the passage as though the Lord said the same thing twice over. But if you follow the figure carefully, you will find that Jesus was absolute Master of metaphor. There was no blunder, and no intellectual inaccuracy in the figures He used. "On this rock," that is the declaration of the impregnable strength of His church against the attacks from without. "I will build," that is an affirmation of the certainty of its perfection and completion. But what follows? The same thing repeated in another form? By no means. "The gates of Hades shall not prevail against it." That does not mean that the church is impregnable against attack, but rather that she is unconquerable when she goes forth to attack. An attacking force never carries its own gates up to besiege a city. If Hades is contemplating an attack upon the church, it will not carry its gates with it. The idea is not that Hades will attack the church, but that the church will attack Hades, and as she does so, the very gates of Hades will yield before her.

Thus we have two declarations about the church by the Master; she is built by Christ on the rock, and when she goes forth on the conquests of Christ, she conquers all intervening foes, and finally the last enemy, the very gates of Hades, shall yield to her. She shall conquer through life, through death, and unto the endless ages. That is the church I belong to, the church impregnable, unconquerable, marching out in perpetual triumph into the ages beyond. That is Christ's estimate of the church.

On a subsequent occasion Jesus mentions the church again. "If thy brother sin against thee, go, show him his fault between thee and him alone; if he hear thee, thou hast gained thy brother. But if he hear thee not, take thee one or two more, that at the mouth of two witnesses, or three, every word may be established. And if he refuse to hear them, tell it unto the church; and if he refuse to hear the church also, let him be unto thee as the Gentile and the publican." That is the church local. It is impossible to tell to the whole catholic church anything between your brother and yourself; but it can be told and it ought to be told to the local church if that brother is refusing to listen. It is a perfect picture of the church's discipline. The church is to be so constituted, a fellowship of souls in Christ, that the wrong doing of one is felt by, and affects the whole; and the purity of the entire church must be maintained, even at the cost of the excommunication of a brother who persists in wrong doing.

Thus we learn from the words of Jesus, that the church is the building of Christ on the rock, that the church is the aggressive force which Christ leads to ultimate victory, that the church within herself is a fellowship exercising discipline, caring for her own internal life, and able to exercise final and Divine authority in the case of all those in membership. These things are true of the catholic church, and also of the local church.

From these first uses of the word in the New Testament it is at once seen that the local church is a model of the catholic church, that all the truths concerning the catholic church are true in measure and in degree of the local church, and if we would understand what the function and the force of the local church is, we shall have to attempt to get a vision of the function and the force of the catholic church.

Now as I pass from these words of Jesus, one or two words concerning the use of the word in the Acts of the Apostles will be in order. In the second chapter of the Acts of the Apostles, and the forty-seventh verse, "And the Lord added to them day by day those that were saved," the word church is inserted in King James' Version. It is not in the original text. Its introduction is of the nature of exposition, and translators almost invariably break down when they attempt exposition. The statement there is that, "the Lord added together them that were being saved," and the translators thought it must be "added to the church." Seeing the word church was not there in the original, the English and American revisers altered it, and put "added to them," that is, to the disciples. That also is only true in a secondary sense. The thought is that He added them to Himself. Of course it is true that when He adds a man to Himself, He adds him to the church.

Through the Acts of the Apostles the word church is used sometimes of the catholic and sometimes of the local church, and the local is always treated as a part and model of the catholic. The actual word ecclesia is used of the congregation of Israel in the wilderness once. In the nineteenth chapter the word is used in the purely Greek sense, "Some therefore cried one thing, and some another: for the *assembly* was in confusion.... But if ye seek anything about other matters, it shall be settled in the regular *assembly*. . . . When he had thus spoken, he dismissed the *assembly*." That word assembly is ecclesia. I am not suggesting that the translation is improper. I think it is wise that the word assembly is used on this occasion. What was the assembly here referred to? It was the gathering together of the members of one particular trade. It is the first record we have, so far as I know, of a trade union meeting, and the word assembly indicates the truth. The reference is not to the great promiscuous crowd which was congregated to see what was going on, but that particular and select number, bound together by a common purpose under a common impulse. The Greek word is there used in its simplest form. It means a called out assembly. It is the assembly of the silversmiths, and it is the assembly of the town government. That is the word ecclesia, in its simple etymological intention.

That word has been taken hold of by the Christian fact, and has become the great word for the church. And it means very simply, an assembly of people, called out, selected from the rest. In the letter to the Ephesians we have a picture of the church in these wonderful words, "There is one body, and one Spirit, even as also ye were called in one hope of your calling; one Lord, one faith, one baptism, one God and Father of all, Who is over all, and through all, and in all." There is nothing in all the New Testament that is more wonderful in its revelation of the nature of the true church. Notice first the apostle describes the church, as "one body." What is the body? Christ and every believer. Not the believers without Christ. The body includes the Head. Of course if we speak of the Head and the body, then for the single moment we mean by the body, all except the Head; but in the statement "there is one body," in this passage the apostle is taking in the whole fact, Christ who is the Head, and all members. "One Spirit," that is the life of the one body, the intelligence of the one body, the emotion of the one body, the will of the one body. "He that is joined to the Lord is one Spirit," so that the whole body of the church is one with the Head, and the Head is one with the body, and that one unifying Spirit of God, in Christ and in all believers, creates the one body. One dominating life that of the Spirit, in Christ and in the believer, unifying Christ and the believer, and all believers with each other, because all are united to Christ.

"One body, and one Spirit, even as also ye were called in one hope of your calling," that is to say, there is one calling for Christ and the believer, for the whole church which is the body. In the former part of the epistle that calling is declared to be that of showing to the ages to come the grace of God, and teaching the principalities and powers in the heavenlies the manifold wisdom of God. That will be the work of Christ and His people forever.

One body, Christ and all the members. One Spirit, filling the whole body up to its last reach. One calling, the eternal calling of Christ in union with the church, and the church in union with Christ. This is a general statement concerning the organism, the life, the calling of the church.

The apostle next shows how individual members become members of the church, how the units enter this living unity. "One Lord," the Object of faith; "one faith," set upon the one Lord; "one baptism," the baptism of the Holy Spirit, that unites the faithful soul with the living Lord. That is the whole process.

The first note in the evangel is that of the Lordship of Christ. Jesus is Lord by virtue of the splendor of His character, by virtue of the victory of His Cross, by virtue of the power of His resurrection. That "one Lord," is presented to the soul as the Object of faith. The answer of faith to the vision of the Lord is the whole of human responsibility. That is the "one faith." Its nature is that of believing on Him, or receiving Him as Lord. It is the act of the will in surrender. That act of faith is responded to by the "one baptism," that baptism of the Holy Spirit whereby the soul believing on the Lord is made a member of the Lord Himself.

Thus the individual enters the church. The one Lord is presented to him. He believes. The Spirit baptizes him, and he is a member. The human responsibility is belief, the Divine answer is the baptism of the Holy Spirit whereby that man is merged into the Christ life, and becomes a member of Jesus Christ. "One Lord, one faith, one baptism."

Thus is He building His Church. Man cannot admit into the catholic church. No one is admitted into the church by water baptism, nor by vote of a church meeting, nor by the decision of a session. A person enters the church when the Holy Spirit baptizes him into Christ. All the other things may be necessary in order that the discipline of the local church may be maintained. There ought to be solemn recognition of some kind when a man joins the outward and visible church, but all such matters are outward and visible recognition of the inward and invisible facts. The only condition on which any person should be admitted to a local church is that evidence is given of membership in the catholic church by the baptism of the Holy Spirit.

Once again, "One God and Father of all, who is over all, and through all, and in all." That is the last fact of the sevenfold unity. It indicates the glorious realization of the purpose and plan of God in His government of, operation through, and union with the ransomed society.

This great church of the firstborn is being built, and as yet man has never seen it. We see parts of it, but the scaffolding is all about it yet; and sometimes it seems as though there were more scaffolding than church. But when He comes, all the scaffolding will go; and the glorious church the firstborn, made up of ransomed souls baptized into the life of Christ, the great entity and unity through which God will manifest Himself to ages and to principalities, will be revealed in all its radiant splendor.

Let us now think of the local church in the light of this. Every church is, as in the catholic church, an assembly of those submitted to the Lordship of Christ. That is the gate, that is the entrance, that is the foundation fact. A local church is herefore an assembly of souls submitted to the Lordship of Christ. That does not tell all the story, but it gives the key to the whole truth. Everything else follows, and to understand that, let us go back to our evangel. The first note is that of the Lordship of Christ. Men submit to that Lordship by believing on Him. Then not only do they see the vision of the Lord, but share the value of His death, and the virtue of His life, and the victory of His presence. In the fifth chapter of Romans we see how these things are realized within the church in the living members who are baptized into union with Christ. The tenth verse, "For if, while we were enemies, we were reconciled to God through the death of His Son, much more, being reconciled, shall we be saved in His life." The seventeenth verse, "For if, by the trespass of one, death reigned through the one; much more shall they that receive the abundance of grace of the gift of righteousness reign in life through the One." "Reconciled by His death," "reign in life." Now as an aid to memory let us take three words, reconciled, regenerate, regnant. These words mark the truth in the case of every individual believer. The individual believer submitted to the Lordship of Christ, is reconciled to God by the value of His death, regenerate by the virtue of His life communicated, regnant by the indwelling Christ through the Holy Spirit.

Now believing that a church is an assembly of such persons, what results follow? Every church is intended to be within itself a manifestation of all the purposes and the facts of the Kingdom of God. A church is an assembly of persons, who in the power of the indwelling life of Christ, realizing the ideals of Jesus, obey the teaching of Jesus, and take part in the activities of Jesus. It is here where perhaps the church has most sadly failed in the past, and where the failure of the church today is most apparent. We have too largely looked upon the negative side, which has to do almost exclusively with such facts as constitute the saving of the individual from sin, and from punishment. These are most important facts. But the great society of God, vitally one, essentially one, socially one, aggressively one, where is it at the present hour? The church ought to be a society accepting the ideals of Jesus, and realizing them in the power of His life; consequently a society of people obeying the moral code of Jesus, and therefore a society of people manifesting to the world the breadth and beauty and beneficence of the Kingship of God in and through Jesus ·Christ. Is that what the church is? That is what the church ought to be, for that is the Divine intention.

But someone will say, What has all this to do with the evangelistic church. And the very fact of the question reveals the weakness of the hour. The church has largely failed in evangelism because the church has not realized within her own borders the force of her own life. We ask how is it that the masses refuse to listen to her evangel, and are treating her in so marked a degree, with contempt? Because the masses see perfectly well that she is not obedient to her own Master's ideals, and does not realize His purpose. That is the severest criticism, and it ought to make us blush, and hide our heads with shame, that the church is not fulfilling her Master's ideals. The evangelistic church is the church which shares Christ's life, and in the power of it obeys His law, and thus manifests Him to the world. Thus alone can the church engage in His work, and carry out His enterprises. When the church realizes and manifests her Lord, in her personal membership, and corporate capacity, then, and then only is she doing His work, the work of seeking and saving the lost. That is the evangelistic church, and that is the true church of Jesus Christ.

The purpose of the church is certainly that of conserving the life of the saints, but this only in order that every saint, and all the saints, may be strong for carrying out the purposes and the work of Jesus Christ. "Ye shall be my witnesses," not witnesses as talkers merely, but evidences, credentials, demonstrations, proofs among men. The only church which is truly evangelistic is the church which realizes within her own borders all the will of her Lord and Master Jesus Christ.

Strength of spiritual life always issues in the manifestation through the church to the world of the facts of the Kingship of God in Christ, and the power of Jesus Christ to deal with all the things in human life that are contrary to the mind and will of God. The church is to be aggressive, capturing men, fighting against wrong, urging everywhere and always the claims of Jesus Christ, and this she can only be as within her own borders there is realized the purposes of God.

In conclusion, the evangelical church is necessarily evangelistic. There are some things so patent they ought not to need stating. Yet there seems to be a prevalent idea that it is possible for a church to be evangelical and not evangelistic. It is not possible. A friend of mine in the ministry, a man of whose scholarship and whose devotion there can be no doubt, talking to me about evangelistic work, accounting for his own lack of interest said, "Well I am profoundly evangelical, but I am by no means evangelistic." There would seem to be many who take that view. Let me say to you, my brethren, that this is an absurd contradiction of terms. No man is truly evangelical unless he is evangelistic also. What did my friend mean? He meant that he held the evangelical doctrines of our holy faith, but he was not interested in the specific work of winning men to Christ. Now what are the foundation doctrines of our holy faith? Evangelical faith affirms the death of Christ was rendered necessary by the ruin of the race, and that it is God's provision for man's salvation. It moreover declares that His life is at the disposal of men for their new life of holiness. Are we evangelical? Do we believe that Jesus died in order that He might save men? If not, then we cannot claim to be evangelical. But if we do, can we seriously assert that holding the doctrines, we are yet content to do nothing for the men for whom Christ died? Knowing that we have the deposit of truth, the great evangel, equal to the salvation of men, are we careless about making it known?

Sometimes one reads an advertisement which declares a sure and certain cure for cancer has been discovered. A man so advertising is wholly despicable. In the first place because the assertion is a lie, but secondly because if it is true, he is a rogue to hold for purposes of personal gain a secret which should immediately be given to the world for the cure of that awful disease. And a man tells me he is evangelical, he holds the truth about salvation, and is thankful to God for the salvation of his own poor miserable soul. I deny it. If the cross of Christ in his own life has meant deliverance, cleansing, purity, that consciousness will drive any man out into evangelistic work and effort.

Evangelism demands a church, and wherever the church of Jesus Christ is, there is an instrument for evangelistic work, because there is a company of men and women in whom the evangel has won its victory, and through whom it is manifested as a life, and proclaimed as a message.

Let me say to all ministers, you will find you must have your church act with you if you are going to do any evangelistic work. And to church members, it is no use wasting breath in the criticism of a minister because he is not doing evangelistic work. Let the church fall into line. One of the first missions of the ministry will be to bring his church into sympathy, and that will often need a great deal of common sense and patience.

No church ought to be allowed to exist that has not added to its membership by confession of faith. If a church is existing only by letters of transfer, it is time the doors were closed, and "Ichabod, the glory of the Lord has departed" was inscribed across them.

This evangelism must begin in the churches. The churches

themselves must be turned back to the work of evangelism. We are trusting too much to organizations outside the church. It is in the church the work must be done. We shall have to travail in birth for the souls of our own people. When in our own church life all the forces of the Christ life are operative without hindrance, then men will be brought under the sound and power of the great and glorious evangel. May God make all our churches, churches after the pattern of the catholic church, "one body, one Spirit, one calling," and "God over, through, in all," moving to His purpose, accomplishing that purpose through the Spirit of Jesus Christ.

THE UNITY OF THE CHURCH

"Neither for these only do I pray, but for them also that be-lieve on me through their word, that they may all be one, even as thou, Father, art in me, and I in thee, that they also may be in us: that the world may believe that thou didst send me."
— John 17:20, 21

DURING RECENT years there have been many unauthorized attempts to bring about what is spoken of as the re-union of Christendom.

These attempts are vain and foolish, for many reasons. First, there has been no disruption of God's church. Secondly, unity has been confounded with uniformity, though they are entirely different. Thirdly, the human divisions and bitternesses, all of them on the surface, have been caused by a forgetfulness of the underlying facts which are wholly Divine.

THERE ARE DIVISIONS AMONG US

I claim to be rather in apostolic succession in this matter, and to say with the great teacher of the churches of old, "Ye are yet carnal." "I hear that divisions exist among you."

I believe that the division of the church of Christ, as to its outward manifestation to the world, is tragic, and that it has hindered the accomplishment of the purposes of God. I am convinced that there is no way of healing these divisions, save by a return to recognition of the first principle of unity, as taught by our Lord. This accomplished, the outward discrepancies may be left to right themselves.

So, in speaking to you upon the great subject of the unity of the church, I do not come with any scheme for re-union; but I do invite you, solemnly and patiently, to

A TWOFOLD CONSIDERATION

First, of the unity of the church as revealed in the intercessory prayer of Christ, which we read together this morning; and, secondly, of an application of the truths of that intercessory prayer to the necessities of the hour.

First, then, the unity of the church as revealed in this intercessory prayer of our Lord. Christ was approaching the last hours of His sojourn upon the earth. The Passion-baptism, of which He had frequently spoken during the later days of His life, was close at hand. Thinking of Him for a single moment as Man, we see Him in these last days, of which we have such a full account only in the Gospel of John, looking into the face of death – of death in its most appalling and awful form, not merely considered within the realm of human suffering, but looking into the face of the one death of humanity. The great word of the Gospel is this, "Christ died," and no other human soul has died in the same sense.

He is facing death, and looking through it, to everything that lies beyond. He stands, the Man of keen, clear, correct, perfect vision, and He knows what will be the unfolding of all that He has done and said in His sojourn upon the earth.

He has delivered His final messages to His disciples, and His final words were, "These things have I spoken unto you, that in me ye may have peace. In the world ye have tribulation; but be of good cheer; I have overcome the world." This is

BUT THE NOTE OF A MAN WHO HAS BEEN BEATEN
but of a perfect Victor, looking right on into the face of His

death, with the thought in His heart, "I have overcome — I have overcome the world."

Then He lifted His eyes to heaven and prayed. That great prayer falls into three divisions. In the first five verses He prays for Himself. You will notice, if you look carefully at the verses, that all the sentences have to do with His relation to His Father, and with His Father's relation to Himself.

Then from the sixth verse the prayer moves on into another realm. He begins now to pray for the little group of men that are round about Him. "I have," He says, "manifested thy name unto the men whom thou gavest me out of the world: Thine they were, and thou gavest them to me; and they have kept thy word." From there to the end of the nineteenth verse He is praying for those men, for His first disciples, for Peter, James, John, and the rest, for the men who were associated with Him in the companionship of His public life.

Then, in verse twenty, we have the beginning of the third section of the prayer, which moves out into the larger realm. "Neither for these only do I pray" — these only, the disciples for whom He had been praying — "but for them also that. . . ." My imagination always takes wings when I read this prayer. I seem to look back to the days of Jesus, and to see Him standing in the midst of those men, having first prayed for Himself, and then for them. I see Him looking at the great host that are coming to Him, the host of the weary and the worn and the sad of earth's sons and daughters, from every people and nation and clime, and, in that great host, He saw me — He saw you. This prayer is wider than His own personality, and goes further afield than that little group of His disciples. It embraces within itself the whole host of God.

"Neither for these only do I pray, but for them also who believe on me through their word," and from there to the end of the prayer we have

PETITIONS FOR THE WHOLE CATHOLIC CHURCH

Now if we carefully bear in mind the construction of the prayer, we shall be helped to understand its main import and most wonderful petitions. The will of Jesus for His people cannot be misunderstood by any who will give quiet, prayerful attention thereto. He goes back, as we have seen, in the opening section, to His own glory before the world was, in union with the Father, and of this glory He had emptied Himself for a season. He is now returning to it, asking that it may be given back to Him. Standing around Him were the men whom He had gathered out of the world, and to whom He had manifested His Father's name; the men to whom He had given the knowledge of the Father, which was within itself, according to our Lord's own teaching, eternal life.

He sees these men — the despised and rejected men of the day, as He was Himself despised and rejected — He sees them as the first of a great host to be gathered out, and to whom the eternal life of knowing the Father through the Son should be given, and for them He prays.

He prays for Himself first, because He is related to them all by His work. He prays for this little group of men around Him, because through them shall pass the message of His life. Then He prays for the gathering crowds; and what does He ask for them? He asks that they may be one.

Now, let us turn and look particularly at this third section of the prayer, and in doing so we shall discover three things concerning

THE UNITY OF THE CHURCH

We shall discover, first, the nature of the unity of the church; secondly, the method of unity in the church; and, thirdly, the purpose of the unity of the church.

As to the nature of that unity, the pattern is declared in the words, "That they may all be one; even as thou, Father, art in me, and I in thee, that they also may be one in us." The unity of His church is after the similitude of the unity that exists between Himself and His Father. In a moment, the whole subject is lifted by these words of Jesus into a realm higher than anything to which we can find a parallel in the whole of nature. They are so simple that there is not within their compass a word of two syllables, yet they reveal the great mystery of the unity of the Persons in the Trinity, and they reveal, moreover, the pattern of the unity of the church of Jesus Christ.

Two persons are mentioned, the Son and the Father, each a Being, yet each forming a conscious element in a greater Being. The Son having His own Personality, the Father having His own Personality, and yet the One conscious of the whole Being of the two. A vital union, a union based upon a life that is, far and away, in its type and thought, beyond anything that we ever touch until we come into this Divine realm. "Thou in me, and I in thee."

Now the Master prays that the church may be united in that way, that the church may be one, made up of separate beings, separate consciousnesses, separate interests, and yet every single person holding within his own consciousness the realization of the whole church.

Surely that has never been realized, or, if so, we have lost it. Also, to a large extent, we have lost it! Isolation, division, and misunderstanding prove that we have lost this great ideal to a tremendous extent; yet the unity of the church is a vital unity after the pattern of the Divine; its members are separate and yet never divided; they possess individuality and personality, and yet, within that individuality and that personality, they are conscious in a measure of the vast whole of which they form a part.

Again, Christ says, "And the glory which thou hast given me I have given unto them; that they may be one, even as we are one; I in them, and thou in me, that they may be perfected into one." The words here, "as we are one," refer to an essential union; or, if I may change the words in order to convey their meaning, to a unity of essence. The unity of the Father and the Son is that of essence; it is not merely unity of consciousness, but unity of nature. Strange as is the mystery to us, and incomprehensible to our finite understanding, yet it remains as the declaration of Jesus, and all we have to do is to

ACCEPT IT FROM HIM WHO IS THE TRUTH

We are not able to follow it in all its bearings; yet we accept it as being the largest revelation that we are able to bear of the union between the Father and the Son. It is not merely a new form of vital union, but it is a unity of essence, so that between them there is no difference whatever.

Upon that is based the idea of the unity of believers – first, with God; and, therefore, with each other. The life that we live is identically the same life. The life you live by faith in the Son of God is the very life that I live by faith in the Son of God. Not only have I a separate identity, but I am sharer of the whole wealth of the life of the catholic church. My life is yours, yours is mine; we are one in essence, if we are Christian men and women. The unity of the church, then, is on the pattern of the unity of the Trinity; and, indeed, is of the same nature.

Take another aspect of this great unity of the church, as revealed in the prayer. Not only is it on the pattern of the Divine unity, but our Lord here reveals to us a threefold progressive unity. Said Jesus, "I am no more in the world, and these are in the world, and I come to Thee. Holy Father, keep them in thy name which thou hast given me, that they may be one, even as we are." Now,

THAT IS THE FIRST ASPECT OF UNITY

It is the unity of the disciples; that is to say, it is the unity of a group of men who are closely associated with each other in Jesus. These men know each other by name, by conversation, by sojourning together, by being fellow disciples; they know the kind of question that each is likely to ask; it is the first circle of acquaintanceship in Jesus Christ. He prays that they may be one. How? "As we are"; that is to say, that this group of men may be one in thought, in purpose, in mind, in service.

That is a prayer, not only for the first disciples, but for every group of disciples from then until now who are associated with each other in local church life. "I pray first for them that they may be one as we are." Into that prayer of Christ, for the company of men who knew each other because of their association with Jesus Christ, we find our place as a church, and every local church is represented there. I am personally inclined to the view that when a church is too large for those of the fellowship to know each other, it should divide. I am very much inclined to think that a church of a thousand members is altogether too large, and that it would be a good thing for half of the members to move on and start another church, and so establish a new center of work. But I will not press this view unduly here and now. I believe that one of the laws for a local church is association of its members with each other in Christ. The Master refers to that as the first sphere of unity.

But again we may find another picture of unity. "Neither for these only do I pray," — that is, for the local company — "but for them also that believe on me through their word; that they may all be one; even as thou, Father, art in me, and I in thee, that they also may be one in us." Here is a slight change of phrase, and I believe it has a wider range of meaning. Christ prayed for the local church that they should be one "as we are"; He prays for the great catholic church, "that they also may be one in us." That is to say, the oneness of the unity of the scattered church is to be a unity of communion with the Father and with the Son —

THAT IS THE UNITY OF THE CATHOLIC CHURCH
So that I am one with the church across the sea, I am one with

the church of two or three, upon the highways of the deep; I am one with my brethren in other communions; I am one with every loyal Christian in this land and the world over.

And how am I one with them? I am one in the communion of the Father, and of the Son, and of the Holy Ghost; "one in us," as the Master said. My unity with my brother far away lies in the fact that he and I will, today, have communion with God and with Christ in the power of the Holy Ghost.

So you have, first, the communion of the local church, of the association of believers who know each other in Jesus, and there the unity is after the pattern of the unity of Father and son, who are one in thought, mind, purpose, and service. Here you have the greater unity of the catholic church upon the earth, "one in us," that is one in communion with the Father and with the Son.

There is still a third phase of union referred to. "And the glory which thou hast given me I have given unto them; that they may be one, even as we are one; I in them, and thou in me, that they may be perfected into one." Now, you have the larger — nay, verily, let me say

THE LARGEST AND MOST PERFECT VISION OF UNITY

Not merely the unity of the local church, of the company of men associated with each other in their association with Christ; not merely the unity of the great catholic church, in communion with the Father, and the Son, and the Holy Ghost; but the coming communion, the coming union, "that they may be perfected." You notice the slight alteration in the Revised Version. The prayer of Jesus is not for the accomplishment of something now, but for the final realization of God's purpose; not that today they may be "perfect in one." Of course, the latter is contained within the other thought; but it is not what the Master prayed for here. He prayed that the whole company, beginning with the Apostles, and running on through every clime, land, age, people, and tongue — those who believed on Him through their word — that at last the whole of them might be perfected into one.

And there the Master who began His prayer with reference to His own relation to the Father, in the past eternities, has reached forward to the coming glory. He sees the great host of the redeemed, gathered from all peoples, tongues, and languages, and He prays, still standing amid the first disciples, that at last the whole church may be perfected into one.

And what a prayer it is! A prayer for the perfection of every member, a prayer for the perfect relationship of one member with another, and, therefore, a prayer for the perfect expression through that finally perfected church of the will and the purpose of the heart of God.

This prayer of Jesus for the perfecting into one of the whole church far outstrips the dream of all the dreamers. Its very magnificence and daring is in itself the declaration of its absolute truth. It was that vision of the prayer of Jesus, I make no doubt, that was in the mind of the apostle Paul when he wrote the letter to the Ephesians, wherein he prays that they might grow up into Christ in all things, "till we all attain" — not each one of us attains, but "till we all attain unto the unity of the faith, and of the knowledge of the Son of God, unto a fullgrown man, unto the measure of the stature of the fulness of Christ."

There, then, we have the threefold glory, the threefold unity of the church. The unity of a local church, a company of men and women associated with each other because associated with Jesus Christ; one "as we are," in mind, purpose, thought, and service; the unity of the catholic church, that communion with the Father and with the son; and the unity of the glorified church hereafter, perfected into one — the great, final, magnificent perfection, reached by the way of the perfecting of individual members.

Now let us consider the method of the unity.

IT IS BASED UPON THE INTERCESSION OF JESUS

"Neither for these only do I pray, but for them also that believe on me through their word" — that embraces the whole church. The intercession of Christ was founded upon His accomplishment of the Father's will and purpose. If we examine the earlier parts of the prayer we shall find that Christ refers to the fact that life eternal had been given to these few men by Himself; that is, the knowledge of the Father, the manifested name. As the prayer proceeds, He says, "I have kept and guarded them in thy name," and He based His prayer for these men upon what He had done for them. Since He prayed the prayer, He has passed through that Passion-baptism. He has been through the waters of death; He has borne our sins in His own body on the tree, and today —

> He ever lives above,
> For us to intercede;
> His all-redeeming love,
> His precious blood to plead.

He still bases His intercession upon His own works, and the unity of the church today is guarded, safeguarded, held inviolate from attacks from without by the intercession of the Son of God.

And then He speaks of this union as being His own gift, the gift of the glory which He had received from His Father, the perfect vision of the Father which transfigures all life by a revelation of the unity of all being.

This He had given them, and it became the very bond of their union.

Then, moreover, union comes by Christ's declaration of the Father's name; the declaration accomplished — "I have made known unto them Thy name"; the declaration progressive — "I will make it known unto them"; and the declaration in its finality — "that the love wherewith thou lovedst me may be in them, and I in them."

Thus hurriedly we have glanced at the method of unity in the church.

Now, lastly, and as briefly,

THE PURPOSE OF THE UNITY OF THE CHURCH

I must recall your minds to careful attention on this point. Why did He repeat it, "That they may be one . . . that they may be one"? "That they may all be one, even as thou, Father, art in me, and I in thee, that they also may be one in us; that the world may believe that thou didst send me." Then, according to this prayer of Jesus Christ the demonstration of the Divinity of the mission of Christ lies in the union of the whole church. Do you wonder that men do not believe in the Divinity of His mission? Do you wonder that the man outside the church says to the one inside, "When you have settled your divisions, then I will talk to you"? Many a Christian man has had that said to him; and do you wonder at it? The possibility of that being said is suggested within the compass of this prayer, "That they may all be one . . . that the world may believe." The miracle is that we see so many people believing, in spite of the breaking up of the unity of the church, in its outward manifestation.

There is yet another reason for true unity, "I in them, and thou in me, that they may be perfected into one; that the world may know that thou didst send me." My brethren, I see very clearly in these two reasons which our Lord gives, the unfolding of a purpose and the declaration of a purpose. First, "that the world may believe." Secondly, "that the world may know." "That the world may believe," — how? By the manifestation of the unity of the catholic church. "That the world may know," — how? By the manifestation of the church perfected into one. So that,

IF WE HAVE MISSED OUR WAY

and we have failed to bring the world to believe by reason of the outward manifestation of internal unity, yet, thank God, the world is to have some other chance; the world is yet to know by the manifestation of the perfection of unity hereafter.

I rejoice this morning, as I ever do, that the great inner fact of unity is in the hands of the King and Priest, and that in the morning that will dawn upon the world, without clouds – that day for which the world waits, amid its sighing and sorrow – when the manifestation of the sons of God, when the perfected unity of the church shall become a blazing fact before the eyes of all men, then will the world not merely believe, but know that God sent Jesus.

What are we to do in sight of this vision of the church's unity? How are we to meet the necessities of the case today? I repeat what I said at the outset: the division of Christendom is a tragic hindrance to the purposes of God. What are we to do? There are three words which I would like to give you to carry away which may help to mark our responsibility today – three words which may help to reveal to us how we may assist in the setting right, in some small measure, of that which is so wrong, according to the prayer and purpose of Christ.

The first word is humiliation. We are a part of the catholic church:

WE HAVE NO RIGHT TO DISASSOCIATE OURSELVES FROM ITS AIMS AND ITS FAILURES

we have a share in the outward breaking up of the Body. The first step to visible unity is that of association in humiliation. It is time that the church of God was upon its knees in confession; it is time that the church of God had done with bungling attempts to tinker up that which is broken into a thousand fragments. It is time that the church went into God's presence, and said, "Lord, the golden bowl of unity is unbroken in Thy hand; but its earthen manifestation we have smashed into a thousand fragments by our selfishness, sin, and folly. We bow in the dust of self-abasement; forgive us."

The trouble is that we do not do that; but we come outside everything else, and we say, "All these are wrong, and we are right." The moment a man does this, the moment a company of Christians take this attitude, what are they doing? Denying their relation to the catholic church of Jesus, cutting themselves off from association with others. We cannot do it. "If one member of the body suffer, the whole body suffers with it." If there is carnality anywhere in the church of Jesus, I must carry its burden, weep beneath the sin of it, cry aloud to the Lord, and say, "Master, we have sinned." If the churches of Jesus Christ would give themselves honestly to humbling before God, then there would come upon us such a sense of the unity that has never been broken as would help us toward a manifestation of it outwardly.

Humiliation is the first word; the second is consecration — not lightly and idly spoken, but in all the great value of the sacred word. If I am to do anything to help the unity of the church in outward manifestation, I must be consecrated; first, to the ideals of Christ; secondly, to the methods of Christ; thirdly, to the purposes of Christ. What are His ideals? The revelation of the Father, through the Son, in the church. What are the methods of Christ? Intercession, the manifestation of glory, and the declaration of the Divine name. And what was the purpose of Christ? That the world may believe. Until side by side with our humiliation there shall take possession of us the great missionary compassion that sees men, far away and near at home,

REALLY PERISHING FOR LACK OF GOD

we can have no share in restoring the unity of the church of Christ. There must be consecration to His ideals, methods, and purpose.

Lastly, there must be co-operation, always and only based upon the foregoing thoughts — humiliation and consecration. Let there be co-operation. I care not whether a man, in humiliation consecrating himself to the ideals of Christ, be in the Roman, the Anglican, the Greek, or the Free churches, that man is one with me, and I with him, and we must help each other. There must be co-operation.

How shall we co-operate? By a view of the sublimities, and by blindness to trivialities. And what are sublimities? The Incarnation — "God was in Christ"; the Atonement — "who gave himself for our sins"; Restoration — "the restoration of all things" as the final issue of Atonement. Oh, that men and women who believe in these things would get together! Blindness to trivialities, what are they? Earthly governments, creeds, opinions, persons — blindness to them all. While the majestic sweep of the Incarnation of God, the Atonement of Christ, and the Restoration of all things holds us — then shall we be near outwardly. In proportion as we gather together in the power of these sublimities, we shall become forgetful of the trivialities, and in some little measure we shall help toward the final fulfilment of the prayer of the blessed Son of God, the great Head of the church, "that they all may be perfected into one." Amen.

THE DOMINION OF MAN

Scripture Reading, Psalm 8

And God said, Let us make man in our image, after our likeness: and let them have dominion over the fish of the sea, and over the fowl of the air, and over the cattle, and over all the earth, and over every creeping thing that creepeth upon the earth. And God created man in his own image, in the image of God created he him; male and female created he them.

— Genesis 1:26, 27

But now we see not yet all things subjected to him. But we behold him who hath been made a little lower than the angels, even Jesus, because of the suffering of death crowned with glory and honor, that by the grace of God he should taste death for every man. — Hebrews 2:8, 9

THE QUESTION of the Hebrew Psalmist is one of the most modern of questions; men are still asking, "What is man?" Yet a distinction must be made in very many cases between the question of the Psalmist and the question which is being asked today. He started with the conviction that man is God-visited. It was that which surprised him. He looked at man and saw at once his littleness and his greatness; his littleness by comparison with the heavens. In the midst of the rhythmic order and wondrous splendor of the universe man seemed but an insignificant atom. Then he looked again, and saw the dignity and the greatness of

man in that the God of the universe visited him, and was mind-
ful of the sons of men. That was the meaning of the Psalmist's
question. In view of this mystery and dignity of so apparently
insignificant a being; What is man? What is the truth concerning this being so small, yet so great, so low, and yet so high, so
much of the dust, and yet of supreme interest to Deity? Such
was the Psalmist's question.

The question today is being asked in quite another mood, and
with quite another emphasis. It is being asked by those who do
not assume that man is God-visited; neither do they admit, in
the answers which they attempt to their questions, that man
is God-visited.

There is no more important question in order to the ordering
of an individual life; there is no more important question in
order to true social conditions; there is no more important question in view of racial adjustment. According to the conception
will be the conduct; according to the conviction which a man
shall have in his own soul concerning himself and his brother
men, will be his behavior as an individual, and in relation to his
brother men.

I propose, therefore, to bring you the Biblical message concerning man, and in the two passages which I have read we find
that message in broad, suggestive, and comprehensive outline.

In the verses from Genesis, so full of poetry, of suggestiveness,
and of beauty, I find the Biblical doctrine as to the place of man
in the Divine purpose; "Let us make man in our image, and
after our likeness: and let them have dominion."

In the brief declaration of the writer of the letter to the
Hebrews I find the Biblical doctrine of the failure of man to
realize that original purpose: "We see not yet all things subjected to him."

And, continuing, we have in the very next sentence the
Biblical doctrine as to the hope of man: "But we behold him
who hath been made a little lower than the angels, even Jesus,

because of the suffering of death, crowned with glory and honor."

First, then, as to this Biblical doctrine of the place of man in the Divine purpose. The Divine purpose for men is that they should have dominion. Man is infinitely more than the last and the highest process of operations entirely within the material. He *is* the last and the highest process of such operations, in certain senses, but he did not become man by such operations and processes. He became man by an act of God, distinct from all other acts; an act by which He did, in the mystery of His wisdom and the operation of His might, differentiate by infinite distances between man and everything that lay beneath him in the scale of creation. According to this declaration of the earliest book of the Bible, celebrated again in the song of the Psalmist, quoted in the holy apostolic writing, God's place for this man in the earth is that of dominion. He made him to have dominion over the whole earth; over all that the earth yields in the mystery of its life; over all that dwelleth upon the earth having sentient life. Over all these, He placed man, that he might have dominion over them. All beneath man is imperfect without him, and can be perfected only as he exercises his dominion.

If you want a commentary on this, open your eyes and look at nature. During the restful and delightful days of my holiday in Scotland, I walked over and over again through one particular estate that for many years had been neglected. How it preached to me! Oh! the glory of it, and the beauty; the rioting of nature; and yet the appalling devastation of it all. Trees, that sprang and grew and came to ripeness, and then were blown down by the tempest; a forest of desolation; the full ripeness of life ruined! Why? Because man had not touched it. Nature needed the touch of the human hand; was waiting for the glory of the master mind; demanded the regency of humanity. That is but a passing illustration. You may see it wherever you look; the earth formed, fashioned, filled with Divine potentialities, waiting for its king; only possible of perfection in any form or fashion by the presence of man. Great forces are hidden in mother earth, sleeping until man shall discover them, and chain them, and make them the messengers of his will, and the instruments of his power. Many discoveries have been made already, but there are others, strange, weird, glorious, waiting for man to discover and use. All the flowers of the field demand the touch of the human hand or they will never come to their ultimate beauty. All the fishes in the sea, and the birds of the air, and the beasts of the earth, God put under man's dominion.

In this passage we have a revelation of that which makes man capable of dominion. "Let us make man in our image, and after our likeness." That is, let us make a being with a mind, able to apprehend, and able to submit; and by that comprehension and submission, able to rule and reign; and thus as the link of connection between the Creator God, and all the things that He has created, they may rise to the fulness of their glory and the ultimate of their beauty. Not carelessly or merely as a matter of rhetoric did the writer of the story say that God said "Let us make man *in our image,*" and *"after our likeness."* An image represents, a likeness resembles, and thus God put over the whole creation a man to represent Him to the creation; and to enable him to do it, he made him like Himself. Man acts for God to the creation, stands to the creation as the representative of God, and that because he is like God.

If the word suggests a being having a mind capable of apprehending and submitting to the authority of the Creator, and, therefore, capable of exercising that authority in the case of all beneath him, it follows that the mind is a spiritual mind, and the power of human government over nature is spiritual and not material. In proportion as a man stands in right relationship with God, knowing Him as the One who commands his life and commands his love, and then stoops to touch the God-created earth, light in a thousand colors will flash from the earth, and life in a thousand manifestations will answer his impress.

This word in Genesis has one other value to which I desire specially to draw attention. When God created man for the purpose of dominion, and gave him power to rule by making him in His own image and after His own likeness, He made him male and female. He created man in His own image, in the image of God created He them. The physical is sacramental. A man is not the complete image of God; neither is a woman. Male and female constitute the Divine image, and there is no perfect unveiling of God save in the unity. I take my way through the mystery and the glory of the Biblical revelation, and I find this truth manifesting itself over and over again. From the Old Testament let me gather two of the most familiar words: "Like as a father pitieth his children, so the Lord pitieth them that fear him." "As one whom his mother comforteth, so will I comfort you." Fatherhood and motherhood are alike homed within God.

Now mark the application of this to the subject of man's place in the universe. Man is to exercise dominion over all beneath him in that unity of being which we speak of as father and mother, all the supreme elements in Deity having their manifestations in each separately, but perfectly only in the union. And how am I to divide between these elements? I know the difficulty of it, for if I speak of certain elements as manifest in man, and certain as manifest in woman, the statement would be in measure inaccurate. All the essential elements of God are found both in man, and in woman; but certain attributes of the Divine shine more clearly in the man, and their complementary aspects more clearly in the woman. The strength and the wisdom of God are manifest through the man, the love and the patience of God are manifest through the woman. Charles Garratt, that poet preacher of the olden days, poetic in his simplicity, said once in my hearing, "God has the arm of the father and the heart of the mother." I do not know that very much can be added to that. That is not to say there is neither love nor patience in a man;

that is not to say there is neither strength nor wisdom in a woman. But it is to say in this great and profound mystery of the creation of humanity according to the Biblical doctrine the elements merging into the fact of Deity are apparent in the way we best can understand under the figure of male and female, fatherhood and motherhood, strength and wisdom married to love and patience. Thus the Biblical doctrine of man is that he has dominion in his dual being, and that for the perfecting of the realm over which he rules there must be the gifts of the male and the female, of the father and the mother, of all strength and wisdom and of all love and patience; the first making the second powerful, the second making the first patient.

We turn from that, all too brief and hurried, survey of the great ideal as presented in the word in Genesis, and we look round. Nay! we first look within, for every human being is in some sense a microcosm of the race. Having looked within we look around, and what are we constrained to say? While in this atmosphere, and in this presence, because we are gathered under the shadow of the cross, we can afford to adopt the patient and tender words of the writer of the letter to the Hebrews, and say this only by way of introduction: "We see not yet all things subjected to him."

Man is not yet in dominion over nature. He has not yet mastered the earth and seas; he has not yet completed his dominion over the yield of the earth in herb and flower and tree. He has not yet mastered the sentient life beneath him. He can tame it, he can slay it, but he cannot rule it. Man is mastered by creation, or else is struggling with it, magnificently struggling with it, heroically struggling with it, struggling with it against fearful odds, but only struggling. Childe Harold declared that man's dominion ends with the shore. The sea laughs back at him and mocks him, at the moment when he thinks he has won his last and ultimate victory. By all this I am not intending to say that nature is incapable of obeying man. In the economy of God the sea is put under the dominion of man; all the mysteries of the earth are intended to obey his behests, and serve him for the fulfilment of his purposes; and all that pass through the paths of the seas, and all that fly in the air, and all that walk or creep over the earth are intended to be under his rule. But we see not yet all things subjected to him.

And why not? Because man has lost his power to rule, because man has lost his sonship, because man has lost his sense of the absolute sovereignty of God. There is a sense in which it is true that man has never ceased to be in the image of God. He is God's representative, to all creation beneath him. Do not be afraid of simple illustrations. Your dog looks upon you as God! And in quite another tone, your little child looks upon you as God! If I were to test any congregation I should discover that Christian men and women in the vast majority of cases climbed by way of their confidence in father and mother to their faith in God. Or else, alas! they were driven from confidence in God by what they saw in them.

Man is in the image of God, but he has lost the likeness. Why has he lost the resemblance? Because he has lost the relationship. Man today is not kingly. His lusts prove it. What are lusts? Panting, passionate desires that cannot be satisfied. That is not kingliness. It was a profound and philosophic word written in the olden days, "Better is he that ruleth his own spirit than he that taketh a city." A man who rules his own spirit knows nothing of lust, nothing of panting, passionate desire. Lust is the panting, passionate cry for something that never comes. That is not kingly. Wars do not demonstrate kingliness, they demonstrate man's inability to be kingly. A man tries to snatch a sceptre by war, and if he does so the defeat of the other proves that the world is without its king; and ere many years have passed, or decades have run their course, the man who snatched the sceptre loses it, as he gained it. Therein is no kingliness. Man is not kingly. Man is weak because he is living wholly within the realm of the material. He has lost his vision, his sense of God. The high aspiration of the soul is not toward God, consequently there is no fine dominion of the mind over all that lies beneath. Man is an enslaved and uncrowned king. We see not yet all things subjected to him.

Administratively this failure of man to have dominion, is due to disruption as between himself and God, and consequently divorce between those parts of the Divine nature, which in their union are intended to exercise a beneficent dominion, resulting in life that is more abounding and ever more beautiful.

And is that the last word of the Biblical doctrine? Nay, verily! All this leads on to the words in which the writer of the letter says, "Now we see not yet all things subjected to him, but we see Jesus."

That is no small word, that is not the turning aside from a massive outlook to something narrow and small. That was the turning of the eye of the writer from the chaos in the midst of which he lived to the focal center of the cosmos. The writer beheld Jesus, and at this point in the letter, I have no doubt that his eyes were turned toward Jesus exalted. And yet, the exaltation of Jesus includes the history of Jesus, and ere we can understand what the writer means when he said, "We see not yet all things subjected to him, but we see Jesus," the exalted One, we must go back and see Jesus, the historic Person. Looking back to Him in human history we see the Man realizing the Divine ideal. "Let us make man in our image, after our likeness." And would we see the man of whom God thought, we must see him in Jesus, the strange human mystery in the midst of human history; the One in whom — mark the paradox — there is neither Hebrew nor Greek; the One in whom there can be neither bond nor free; the One in whom there is neither male nor female; the One in whom the Hebrew is at home and the Hellenist also; who revealed the meaning of the cross and sacrifice as the way into life; who revealed the meaning of culture by beauty and life realized; the One who never bent His neck to any yoke; the One who always bent His neck to the only yoke of the Divine will so that He could not be free; the One in whom there can be neither male, standing alone in the arrogance of his manhood, nor woman alone in the pain or the pride of her womanhood; the One in whom man, with all his strength, and woman, with that yet more wonderful strength of compassion and tenderness, have found their final and their last home. We see Jesus, the strange Person in the midst of human history, the Man of the seamless robe, without a sceptre, without a diadem, without a Parliament, without a program, puzzling and baffling the last Hebrew prophet in his prison because He was conducting no campaign, moving quietly through life, God's norm, the arche-typal Man, Master of the earth, and in His manhood prevailing with wondrous mastery. Seas! He will walk across them! The earth is His, He knows its glory and all its secrets in His man-hood and apart from His Deity! The sustenance of human life that earth will yield to men, bread, He will provide so that multitudes are fed! That which maketh glad the heart of man, the fruit of the vine, He will create at a marriage feast! When fisher folk are beaten He knows just where the fish are, and if they drop the net at His command, they will catch them! When after the lone vigil of forty days in the wilderness has run its course, He stands pure and undefiled, the wild beasts were with Him! You are not to pity Him, but to envy Him. That is not the picture of marauding beasts and the man afraid, but of beasts finding their Lord and Master and lying down with Him. The wild beasts were with Him. God's Master Man, Master of the cosmos, having dominion, and because of such dominion, mag-nificently, I had almost said superciliously independent of the trappings that men wear and think they are dignified. What did He need with a palace or a robe or a sceptre to make Him King? By these things men never become kings; by these things they become uncrowned. He passed for one brief generation in the world's centuries across the stage of human history; God's Man, God's King, bowing to the eternal will, holding communion with the spiritual world, and in the power of that submission mastering all the earth! We see not yet all things put under man, but we have seen Jesus!

Yes, but more, and infinitely more. "We see him crowned with glory and honor, that by the grace of God he should taste death for every man." That is an involved and mystic sentence, reading many ways, and offering many lines of thought. Its simplest meaning is that He was crowned with glory and honor in order that He might die. Mark it well, the supreme crown upon the brow of Jesus was the crown of thorns; the supreme dignity and glory which God conferred upon Him was the glory of dying for others. In the great intercessory prayer in John, He said "Father, the hour is come; glorify thy Son." In those words He asked for the consummation of His life in sacrifice. He prayed also for restoration to the glory from which He had come forth; but He prayed first for the immediate glory and dignity and splendor, of the right to die for men. "No man taketh my life from me. I lay it down of myself; and if I lay it down, I will take it again. This commandment I received of my Father, and therefore my Father loveth me because I lay down my life for the world." He was crowned with glory and honor that He might die.

Oh, God! and Oh, my soul! how little do I know of Christ. And how little do I know of fellowship with Him! How constantly I sigh for the glory that God has for Christ; but how prone I am to forget that His supreme glory was the glory of the cross. The Man who was the norm of humanity, by a mystery that goes far out beyond our explanation, bent Himself to the storm and hurricane; gathered into the mystery of His own personality the virus and prison of sin; and, in one death-grapple in the darkness with the forces that had robbed man of his sceptre, mastered them.

It would almost be an insult to speak of that as heroic. That is beyond heroism; it is Godlike; it is vast as the universe; profound as the nature of God. No man ever dreamed this. Such dignity was not evolved out of human consciousness. It is the nature of the Eternal. But did He win? The answer is in the same declaration, for we see Him, not only crowned with the glory and honor of the right to die, but crowned with the glory and honor that result from the dying. That is the final fact in the Biblical doctrine of man; that Jesus, in the perfection of His humanity, the norm of humanity, in the mystery of His dying, died for every man, and that He is the eternal Man, the age-abiding Man.

Let us beware how we allow false philosophies to rob us of the foundations of our faith. Let us beware of this modern vaporizing, which in its attempt to explain everything, cannot accept either resurrection or ascension. If our New Testament teaches anything, if our Bible teaches anything, it teaches that at the right hand of God, is the Man of Nazareth, at this very hour, corporeal in God's heaven; that He is spiritual nevertheless; and that He is sovereign. By way of the incarnation God did take unto Himself for abiding and eternal union our humanity, in a mystery that is mightier and a glory that is greater than that of creation.

> In Him the sons of Adam boast
> More blessings than their father lost.

We see the Man at the right hand of God, and beholding Him, what do we see? Let the writer of the letter tell his own story. He says of Him, that He is the effulgence of the Divine glory, that He is the very image of His substance. In that same introductory word we have also the story of His victory. "Upholding all things by the word of His power, when He had made purification of sins, sat down on the right hand of the Majesty on high." There we have the whole of the facts of the ministry of Christ revealed. Behold the Man, and beholding

Him, what see you? The effulgence, the out-shining, and the very image of the substance of the Deity. Beholding the Man, what see you? We see Him in public ministry, by word spoken and miracle wrought, upholding all things by the word of His power. That is not a reference to the cosmos, but to the moral order; He insisted upon the spirituality of the material, denying the base doctrine that humanity is dust, or that the world itself is matter only. Upholding all things by the word of His power. And then what? Passing to the mystery of the cross, making purification of sin. And then what? Sitting down at the right hand of the Majesty on high, having regained the sceptre man had lost, to hold it on man's behalf. We see not yet all things subjected, but we see Jesus! We see Him as the crowned Man, the glorified and eternal Man. We see Him having through the mystery of His death won a victory on behalf of humanity. We see Him now, therefore, proceeding to the renewal of men in order that they may regain their dominion.

All this Paul also saw when he wrote the Roman letter. "The whole creation groaneth and travaileth in pain together until now ... waiting." Waiting for what? For God's Man; for the manifestation of the sons of God. This creates the breadth and the grandeur and the glory of Christian work. The winning of a man to Christ is not the winning of a man from interest in the world or power within it. It is the winning of a man that he may get back to his sceptre and govern. As yet we are only at the twilight dawn of the day that is to be. How God will usher in His final day, who shall say? But the day of light and glory that shines under all the fogs that o'erspread our minds, will be the day of the redemption of the cosmos, because the sons of men have become again sons of God.

Finally, to be personal and individual, let me go back to the thing I said at first. Every individual life is a microcosm of the whole. Then how is it with myself? If I explain myself by the light of God's revelation, then, I say first of all, there is need to think well of myself. I am finding in my dealing with men today, not only that men do not know that they are sinners, but almost a profounder malady, that they do not think that God created them, that they do not know they have been made in the image and likeness of God.

I call you back, my brother, from your philosophic speculations. You may return to them presently. I call you back from them for a moment, and I pray you at least let the light of the Biblical declaration fall upon your life. You are created in the image of God, and after the likeness of God. That is the supreme dignity and the supernal glory of human life. I know it well; the image is defaced; and the likeness not manifest! And yet this self, this ego, is not the offspring of hell, but of heaven! I am not the last accidental result of the upheaval of mud! I am of the Divine breath, and the Divine creation. It is when a man knows that, that he knows he is awfully, appallingly of the dust. It is when I see the glory of the Divine intention, that I come to a keen and agonizing sense of my own human failure. I have blighted the flowers, and ruined the birds, and harmed the children! That is the tragedy! I, who should have reigned in rightness and in love, and helped God to fulfil the meaning of His own creation, making the desert blossom as the rose, I have done the work of destruction and devastation, because in myself I am away from Him.

Is there no hope for me? Blessed be God, there is! Behold the Man! Behold Him, wounded, stricken, afflicted; and behold Him triumphant over the dark mystery of death; and behold Him seated at the right hand of power, the prophecy of my realization of the Divine purpose, if I will but crown Him, trust Him, obey Him. Then let me to His cross; let me to His open side;

> Rock of ages, cleft for me,
> Let me hide myself in Thee.

THIS DARKNESS

Our wrestling is not against flesh and blood; but against the principalities, against the powers, against the world rulers of this darkness, against the spiritual hosts of wickedness in the heavenly places — Ephesians 6:12

I propose no academic discussion of this text, but rather a practical and immediate application of its teaching. We are all conscious of the strangely weird appeal of its suggestions; and this the more as we remember that the man who wrote these words was no dreamer haunted by fantastic notions, and incapable of seeing the near things of life actually and wholesomely. The whole paragraph from which the text is taken follows one in which the apostle had been contemplating the home, and dealing with such practical matters as those of the relations between husbands and wives, parents and children, servants and masters. Paul was pre-eminently practical; but he saw life as not wholly accounted for or conditioned by the things seen. To him, as his Philippian letter makes quite clear, all the things of truth, of honor, of justice, of purity, of loveliness, of good report, the things of virtue and the things of praise, resulted from human thinking guarded by the peace of God in Christ Jesus. And so also he saw the conditions of evil, graphically described in our text by the pregnant phrase, "this darkness," as resulting from the destructive rule of spiritual wickedness.

Now it is to this view of life that I desire to draw attention at this time; and that in order to a clearer understanding of its bearing on the calamitous situation in which we find ourselves today, which surely we may describe as "this darkness." In a few brief sentences I propose to attempt first to set before you this apostolic conception; then to consider the present manifestation of his truth; and all so that we of the faith of Christ may understand what our wrestling is, the nature of our conflict in such an hour as this.

First, then, as to the apostolic conception. The central description of conditions is discovered in that brief phrase already twice recited, "this darkness." The phrase arrests by its very bluntness and incompleteness. It suggests life without light; it suggests men looking but without seeing; it suggests obfuscation, spiritual and moral. This darkness!

In the next place observe the revelation of the cause of the darkness contained in the phrase, "the spiritual hosts of wickedness in the heavenlies." The word "hosts" is supplied by the translators. Quite literally we may translate the spiritualities, or the spirituals, the reference being, as the context makes quite clear, to spiritual beings. These spiritualities are described as of wickedness; and the particular word that is translated wickedness here describes evil, not in its inherent quality, but as malignant, harmful, destructive.

These spiritual beings of malignant and harmful and destructive nature are then referred to as being in the heavenlies, a phrase which simply means inhabiting a realm beyond the earthly, not limited as man is for the moment by local conditions and geographical situations; but moving in that spiritual realm, by which man is so closely surrounded, and yet of which, by reason of his flesh, he is so seldom conscious. Spiritual beings of malignant power in the heavenlies are described as having access to the spirit nature of humanity, dealing with those mental capacities out of which all things proceed.

These beings are the world-rulers, as we translate the one word in the apostolic letter. The word means that these beings have seized upon the world, are governing its thought, and so directing its enterprise.

Thus, working backward through the description, we come to the first words, principalities and authorities; words which suggest rank, system, and method in this mystic world of evil spirits which have access to men's souls, and master and determine human thinking.

According to the apostle, the darkness of which he was conscious was the result of the fact that these evil spiritualities had seized upon the world, and were dominating its thought; and the inspirations of human activity were the suggestions made in the secret places of human life by these evil forces.

Such, then, with an almost uncouth but necessary brevity, is the interpretation of the text in itself. Let me attempt with yet greater brevity to express the meaning of it in the language of our own times. The apostle here recognizes the fact that the apparent is the result of the hidden. To quote from the New Testament, in another connection, something that has another application, but the philosophy of which is patent here also— "What is seen hath not been made out of things which do appear." The apostle recognizes the fact that if we would understand any human situation we must get behind the actual appearances of the moment and discover the inspirational centers from which these things have sprung. He recognizes that the natural is always the expression of the supernatural. I have used these words, *natural* and *supernatural,* in our common way, both of them needing to be safeguarded from popular abuse. The natural, that is that which we see, and think we understand, and can account for; this, the apostle declares, is always the expression of what we call the supernatural; that is that which we cannot see, which we do not seem to understand, which we cannot always account for. Out of that general statement of the philosophy of apostolic thinking, we deduce the one application that material calamities always result from spiritual malignity; that the things that create the darkness of this hour in which we live, appalling us with its horror, are the dark things that have been at work for long years. The profoundest calamity is not the immediate clash of battle and shedding of blood, but the mental dislocation and spiritual corruption that lie behind these things; that have made them not only possible, but necessary, and now actual. The warfare of the Christian church is in that spiritual realm. In this very hour of physical conflict she needs to understand her spiritual foes, and so to adjust herself that she may be the instrument of God against the things that make such calamity possible.

Let us now confine ourselves to that which is immediate and pertinent, to the burden that is on our hearts, the calamity that assaults our faith. Let us consider, in the light of this passage, first, what are the inspirations of war, and then let us give attention to the psychosis of war, or the mental derangement that it occasions.

What are the inspirations of war? I wonder how many have seriously taken time to ask the question, "Whence come wars?" The march of every army, the mobilizing for war, and all that we are almost sure, presently, to hear and know of slaughter and of the shambles, have sprung out of human thinking. Apart from human thinking, these things could never be. Feeling one's way back then, honestly, to the original inspiring motive, not for the moment referring to any one nation or to any one man, we are bound to say that all war springs out of the lust for power. I admit that under certain conditions, and in certain circumstances, men speak of prestige; under certain conditions and in certain circumstances they speak of honor — using the word too often in an abused and degraded way. At the back of everything there is lust for power. War has always been the outcome of it. In the day of battle there may be two opposing nations, or forces, or men, both of them actuated by this lust of power; or, on the other hand, war may be caused by one nation's lust of power, and the necessity for resisting that lust for power on the part of other nations. Therefore, there may be an element of righteousness in the conflict. But even then, the beginning is the same; not on the part of those who are driven into the conflict as against their will, but on the part of those who are the aggressors. The origination of war in the human mind is lust for power.

The trouble is that this statement does not stagger the soul as it ought to do. And why not? Because we have not yet thoroughly apprehended the meaning of or believed in the declaration of Christ when He said, speaking for Himself and for His own, that the secret of greatness and fitness for the Kingdom of God is not power exercised over some one else, but service rendered to some one else.

I take a step further. If that be the inspiration of war in the human mind, proceeding out of it in the human conscience is the denial of morality. First there is a philosophy of denial, sometimes clearly formulated, at other times not formulated, but always existent. When there is a denial of morality, then immediately there is an apotheosis of brute force.

Here, because I have to deal with matters of the hour, I am compelled to take an illustration. That great nation of Germany, to which we owe so much for its scientific investigation and its wonderful learning, has, for more than a generation, been under the influence of a philosophy that has denied that reality of the moral. The philosophy of Nietzsche may be condensed into this one brief sentence – "Nothing is true. Everything is permitted to the strong." When that is believed subconsciously by a people, it comes out sooner or later into actuality. At the back of a passion for war, wherever it exists, is this denial of morality. According to the apostolic interpretation, all this proceeds from the influence of the spiritualities of wickedness, and human submission thereto. These movements of mind and attitudes of soul result in ghastly ingenuity for the destruction of human life in order to the obtaining of power. Pride, and hate, and frauds are the things that lie at the back of war. Our nation today is compelled to war in the interest of righteousness, but the occasion of the necessity has been created by an inspiration entirely evil.

The cleanest place in the war of 1914 will be the field of blood, where men, heroic and daring, fall and die! The most corrupt place is the spiritual darkness in which these shambles were made possible. There is the true region of horror; and into that realm the church is called, in order to grapple with the forces of evil that have made the actuality possible and even necessary, and in order that the thing that all men are saying in one way or another may be true: Never again can this thing happen! The trouble is that even we, who name the Name of Christ, too often shudder in the wrong place. To take this vast and ghastly business and illustrate it in the microcosm of individual experience — we shudder when the murderer is arrested with the blood of his victim upon his hand. God shudders at the first movement in his soul that makes the murder possible. Jesus said, "It was said to them of old time, Thou shalt not kill; but I say unto you that there is to be in the heart neither contempt nor anger, and then murder will be impossible!" To return from that microcosm of individual experience to this microcosm of shame and agony, let us remember that the place where we ought to shudder and blanch with fear is in the presence of the spiritual and mental derangement that has made this thing possible! There our fight must be fought. Our wrestling is not against flesh and blood but against principalities and powers; against the world-rulers of this darkness, the spiritualities of malignant intention in the heavenly places.

Now for practical purposes I want to speak of the psychosis of war. Let me immediately say that that is a phrase I should not have used for myself. I have borrowed it. I have borrowed it because it arrested me. I will not use it many times.

A correspondent in one of our great papers recently, speaking of the false rumors that are being spread on every hand, told how some sailors during the last few days gave a very definite description of something which they declared had happened in front of their eyes. As a matter of fact, it never happened at all! The writer, having told the story, said, "That is the psychosis of war."

It was a revealing phrase. It showed me that this man, whosoever he may have been, was a man understanding something of the peril of the hour. Let me drop the phrase of the writer, translating it into language understood more of the common people. What does it mean? The mental derangement which results from war.

Here let me first of all say how profoundly I thank God for the little manifestation there has been, not in our own land only, but also in France and Belgium, of anything like passion, of anything like widespread mental derangement. Having said so, it is well that we recognize that there is something weird and mysterious in the influences developed by such an hour of terrible tension as this, and in the effects resulting upon the human mind.

We all need to watch, and supremely those who are to be the guardians of others, for in such an hour as this there is the danger of the overclouding of the intellect, and the consequent distortion of truth. It becomes difficult to see clearly the real causes, to trace the true course, to forecast the inevitable consummation. This strange obfuscation of the understanding will have its manifestation in things we say of each other, and things we write in our magazines and newspapers about our enemies; about victories that we are supposed to have won; about defeats that we are supposed to suffer. There is a strange obliquity of vision that in an hour like this puts the whole of us in danger of being untrue. Even a brilliant man may write a poem and publish it in a great newspaper, which entirely misrepresents the truth concerning the German nation.

Again, in such an hour as this the whole emotional life of the people is in danger. The strain and stress of this awful time tends to arouse passion in many directions; tends to the stirring up of hate, tends to the stirring up of affection. If we have open eyes, we cannot walk our streets today without being profoundly conscious of the dire and ghastly perils that are threatening our people, and especially our young people. They may be unable to account for it, are hardly conscious of it — nor desiring it; but the very strain and stress of the hour is proving a stimulus to the emotions which is putting life in grave peril. There is a strange and subtle and terrific incitement to impurity abroad in the land at this hour. None can come at all into close touch with young life, beautiful young life, sympathetically and sanely into touch with it, without feeling that the hour is an hour of tragic peril. It is an hour in which there is born within the consciousness of man a passionate craving for narcotics or stimulants as the case may be. The life of the nation is weakened in its moral fiber; the volitional powers of men are weakened by the darkening of intelligence, and by the fever of emotion.

These effects are produced principally upon those who are not called to physical conflict, and upon those who are so called, before they actually are face to face therewith. Let me read a few brief sentences from one of our weekly papers;

> It is the psychology of war-passion, not in the combatants, but in the obsessed and absorbed spectators, that needs most careful watching, lest a sudden collapse of intelligence and *morale* should plunge our people into a debauch of reckless, unreasoning brutality of feeling and conduct which will impair, perhaps ruin, those resources of clear judgment and effective cooperation upon which the successful conduct of such a struggle as that on which our national safety hangs must in the long run chiefly depend. The symptoms of this terrible disease are well known, the

coming of violent language into blind hate and suspicion, the alternation of vainglory and profound dejection, a credulity so intense as to produce an automatic acceptance of every statement favorable to our side and every statement damaging to the enemy.

In these realms, we discover the real places of the church's warfare. The church must stand confronting the nation, herself strong in her faith, strong in her courage, profound in her conviction of the established Throne of God, and the infinite rectitude of the Divine government, and the profound compassion of the Divine heart; and by the dignity and heroism of her conduct she must help to save the nation from the assaults of these spiritual hosts of wickedness which poison life at the springs of thought and conception, and make calamities more terrific than the bloodshed on the field of battle!

Our wrestling must be in that region. Here is the supreme danger of the hour; and here, therefore, for the church, is the opportunity of the hour. Our sons are going forth to war! Oh! the pity of it! Oh! the shame of it! Yet the necessity for it we see! If we at home, who are shut up here by reason of our vocation, and by reason of our responsibilities, are inclined to say and to imagine that we have no part in the conflict, that we cannot render any service, we are mistaken! We can render magnificent service by living our own personal lives in such simple fashion as not to create panic in the matter of the necessities of life. Moreover, we can serve this crisis in our national history, this world-crisis, in no better way than that of entering into this spiritual conflict. How shall we do it? I shall ask you at your leisure, who really are considering such a question as this, to read anew that whole passage in Ephesians, beginning with the phrase, "Finally, my brethren!" First, in one inclusive word, we find the whole secret of conducting this warfare. This is it: "Be strong in the Lord, and in the power of his might." This is the hour of all hours in which private prayer must not be neglected;

and private devotional study of the Word of God must not be laid aside. We must cultivate our own spiritual life. We must be strong in the Lord. The apostle goes on to show what that means, "Put on the whole armor of God!" "Take up the whole armor of God!" "Put on the panoply of God!" This does not mean, first, the armor which God provides for us. It means first the armor God wears, the armor that makes Him invincible, the armor, wearing which, His Throne is still established!

The armor of God! What is it? We will not stay for detailed examination, but take the essential things: Truth, Righteousness, the Evangel of Peace, Faith, Salvation, the Word of God! These are the things in which we shall be strong in the Lord, and in the power of His might.

We must enter into this warfare by getting into grips with the foe; by putting ourselves in evidence as against anything and everything which tends to weaken the moral fiber of our people, or to disturb their mental and spiritual strength; by allowing our life to have natural and definite action not merely in great occasions and great deeds, but in the tones and tempers of all our days; by seeking close comradeship with the tried and the distressed; by standing side by side, in sane and happy fellowship, with those who may be in peril. I solemnly affirm — and I would God I could say this so that it might be heard and believed — the whole church of God, at this hour, ought to be at the disposal of the nation for ministry within this spiritual realm. It is the hour when every minister should be at his post, when every Sunday School teacher should be meeting his or her class, when every mothers' meeting should be held, when all our agencies should be conducted with cheerfulness and confidence, in order that we may inspire the nation with these highest spiritual elements of courage, apart from which we shall deteriorate under this catastrophe of war.

Moreover, the church at this hour must inspire the rulers wherever the opportunity occurs. A very little way from the doors of this sanctuary something happened recently that was symbolic. Some of our soldiers were in a public-house at about 10:30 at night. The hour for closing that public-house is 12:30. But at 10:30 the proprietor of that house persuaded them that it was time to close, and got them across the threshold. As soon as they were away, he shut the doors on his own initiative, two hours earlier than necessary. Our nation ought to do that, and not merely the individual publican, at this hour. That is only one practical illustration.

In a business house in this city, a man, apparently a gentleman, asked one of the girls whether there might be some difficulty coming in the matter of wages. She told him yes, and he offered her the phone number of his club privately, that she might let him know if she were in any difficulty. A godly man was told that story, and he said the girl must be overwrought! That was not so. She was a sane, sweet, strong girl, whom I personally know. London is full of that possibility just now. The devil will take full advantage of the opportunity he has created. The church of God must stand by all such lonely souls; open her halls to receive them, and put her resources at their disposal. These are practical illustrations. It is only as our eyes are open to see them that we shall get down to our true business today. We are wrestling in that realm, and it is ours to hold the fort today with spiritual courage and moral strength and mental sanity; and as we do so we make one of the greatest contributions that can be made to the hour of terrific crisis.

One word more. Those of you who are familiar with your New Testament in the Greek will recognize when Paul wrote, *"We wrestle,"* he introduced into a military figure a word which is not military. It is the word of the athlete. Why did he do this? I think he did so in order to suggest that this conflict must be individual. Therefore I charge you, my brother, my sister — wheresoever you may live, and wheresoever you may serve in this crisis — get into personal grip with these spiritual forces that blight and blast by poisoning the intellectual faculty, the emotional forces, the volitional power of humanity. By your courage and your faith and your love, and by the ministry you are able to render to suffering people, until the calamity shall be overpast, and we shall find our way into something cleaner, brighter, better — help your nation, and fight in company with God!

DISCIPLES FOR BUILDING AND BATTLE

Luke 4:25-35

For which of you, desiring to build a tower, doth not first sit down and count the cost, whether he hath wherewith to complete it? — Luke 14:28

Or what king, as he goeth to encounter another king in war, will not sit down first and take counsel whether he is able with ten thousand to meet him that cometh against him with twenty thousand? — Luke 14:31

H ERE ARE two questions, both of them moving in the figurative realm, and we can only understand their value as we keep them in their context. The paragraph is arresting for many reasons. The story in which it is found occupies Luke 14, 15, 16, and 17:1-10. In these chapters we have the account of a Sabbath afternoon in the life of Jesus, and, as a matter of fact, the last of which we have any account in the course of His ministry. It tells us how He accepted the invitation of one of the rulers of the Pharisees to eat bread with him, and going into the house of that ruler, He did perhaps the most unconventional things that He ever did. When He came out, Luke tells us that there went with Him great multitudes. No man can read these narratives of the life of Jesus without being impressed with the fact that everywhere He attracted men and women to Himself. I am not saying that they all obeyed Him or that they crowned Him. I am only referring to His supreme and superlative attractiveness. When He left this house, evidently beginning to walk along the

179

way, His face being set toward Jerusalem on the final journey, the people got up from where they had been waiting, and moved after Him. Luke tells us that He turned, and facing the crowd of people that were eager to follow Him, loving to be with Him, waiting to hear anything He might have to say to them, most keen to see any work that He might work, He uttered the terms of discipleship, the most searching and severe that ever fell from His lips. I read them to you. I am not going to read them again, but you remember them. If we are perfectly honest, and of course, we are going to be that in the House of God, we shall admit that as we read them or heard them read terror filled our hearts. Or were you not listening when I read them, or were you imagining as I read them that you knew them, and therefore you could think about what you would do in the city tomorrow? That is the trouble, you know, with our worship. I never read them, as God is my witness, without wondering if I am a disciple at all.

He told that listening crowd that whereas they were attracted to Him, eager to follow Him. wanting to hear Him, loving to watch Him, desiring in some way to be identified with Him, it was impossible for any man to be His disciple unless that man should put His claims above the highest and holiest and best things of earthly life and relationship. I need not insult the intelligence of this audience by reminding you that when He speaks here of hating father and mother, wife, child, brother, sister, life, He is not saying that the necessity for discipleship is malice in the heart against such. He is simply indicating the fact not that low things and vulgar things are to be given up, but that high things and holy things and beautiful things, the most beautiful things of the world, the love of father, of mother, of wife, of child, of brother, and sister, and the love of life itself, if the hour shall ever strike when there is a conflict between loyalty to Him and these high loves, these are to be trampled underfoot.

Then he uttered the second of His terms of discipleship. He

said that no man can come after Him and be His disciple unless that man is prepared to take up his own cross and follow Him. Then He gathered up these two and said, Except a man renounce all that he hath, he cannot be My disciple.

These are His terms of discipleship. You notice that I did not say they *were*. They *are*. They abide. Christ never told any man that it was going to be easy to be a Christian. That blasphemy against eternal things is the outcome of a misunderstanding of Christ's message.

Between the enunciation of the two terms and their recapitulation in the form of one, I find the two verses I have read. He said, "Which of you, desiring to build a tower, doth not first sit down and count the cost, whether he hath wherewith to complete it? ... Or, what king, as he goeth to encounter another king in war, will not sit down first and take counsel whether he is able with ten thousand to meet him that cometh against him with twenty thousand?"

What did our Lord mean by these two questions and these two suggestions? He was appealing to His listeners, the men and women who were hushed into silence, and I cannot but believe, subdued and solemnized in great fear at His terms. To them He said, Which of you going to build a tower, or what king going to make war. He was talking to His hearers, and I have no hesitation in saying, though I have not the authority for it as a documentary statement, that He saw upon the faces of that crowd exactly the protest that is in my heart when I hear these terms of discipleship. He knew what they were thinking. I will try to interpret to you their thinking. They were thinking and saying in their hearts something like this: Oh, Jesus, prophet of Nazareth, we have followed Thee a long while, we love Thy wonderful teaching, we love the tenderness of Thy dealings with humanity, we would like to be identified with Thee, but we are filled with terror when Thou makest Thy terms of discipleship so severe! Why not make it easier for us? Why ask us to trample under foot the high loves of earth, in order to be loyal to Thee, if necessary. Why ask us to take up the cross? Cannot it be easier? Is there not some easier way of discipleship than that? He saw the protest on their faces, He explained to the wistful crowd the reason for the severity of His terms. He said, Which of you building a tower doth not first count the cost? Which of you going to battle but does not consult as to the quality of his soldiers? By which He did not mean, that *they* were to count the cost. He never told men they were to count the cost. He told them they were to come after Him without counting the cost, they were to come at all costs, that if a man would come after Him, if his right hand offend, he must cut it off, or his eye cause him to stumble, he must gouge it out.

Then what did He mean? He meant that He had to count the cost. He was the builder. He was the warrior. He was appealing to these men to put themselves in His place; as though He had said to them, You are protesting in your heart against the severity of My terms. Do not you understand Me? Suppose you were in My place, which of you going to build a tower, would not count the cost? Supposing you were in My place, which of you, as a king going to war, would not be concerned with the quality of your soldiers? My terms are severe, because I want men and women as disciples who will stand by My side until the building is done, until the fight is won. That is the reason for the severity of His terms.

That being so, let us reverently consider some things revealed. First, we discover our Lord's conception of His own work in the world. That work, as suggested by His two figures of speech, is that of building and battle. That is consonant with the whole Biblical revelation. Six months before this, at Caesarea Philippi, when Peter made his great confession that Christ was the Son of the living God, Jesus said to him, "On this rock I will build my church — building — and the gates of Hades shall not prevail against it" — battle. In other words, the mission of Christ is re-

vealed suggestively in these figures of speech as being Constructive and Destructive. He came into the world for building, and
because there are forces that prevent the building, He came into
the world for battle. If we stand back a little further from the
record, that we may have a larger view, we find that the whole
story of the Bible is the story of God in human history building,
and in battle. The constructive is the ultimate in the purpose of
God, but the destructive is necessary in the process. The Bible
opens in a garden. Where does it end? In a city. The Bible is
the story of God's process from the Garden to the City. His de-
termination to realize the ultimate meaning of humanity as it
can only be expressed in the city. Man is also seen all the way
trying to build his city, the passion for it being inherent in the
human soul, but he has not yet built a city that is worth living
in, not even London. Garden cities are approximating to the
divine ideal, but there are no garden cities that are perfect yet,
but they are going to be. God's City will be a garden city, and
into that ultimate city all the nations shall bring their glory and
their honor. It is only God-built, and all the way fighting is
necessary, fighting against the obstructive forces that prevent or
postpone the building of the city.

Charles Haddon Spurgeon called his Magazine *The Sword
and Trowel.* What made him do that? The idea was taken from
Nehemiah, and he knew that in Nehemiah you have revelation
of abiding principles. Nehemiah in building the walls of the city,
had a sword in one hand and a trowel in the other. So he built.
Thus Nehemiah is a wonderful illustration of the work of God
in the march of the centuries, ever building and always at war.
Jesus came into the world, and He said on a memorable occasion,
"My Father worketh hitherto and I work."

Therefore, said Jesus in effect: You make protest in your
heart and mind and will against the severity of My terms. I tell
you why they are severe. I am in this world to do battle, and I
am in this world to build, and the ultimate passion of My heart

is the building, and the present necessity of My mission is the battle. Therefore I need disciples who will stand by Me till the building is done, and the battle is won.

Christ is far more concerned in the fulfilment of God's enterprise in the world, with the quality of His disciples than with the quantity. Let no man misunderstand me. If it be a matter of ultimate salvation, He is concerned with quantity, for God loved the world, and there is no human being outside the sweep and scope of the divine love or the purpose of the redeeming Lord. But He is seeking fellow workers, and therefore He is far more concerned, I repeat, with quality than with quantity. We need either to discover this afresh, or to rediscover it. We are cursed today with a passion for statistics. I find it all round the world. People will say, "Look at this chapel tonight. That is a fine success." Not necessarily so. There are other chapels where only a handful of souls have gathered, and yet perhaps in the records of eternity we shall find that more mighty work for God is being done there than here.

In the Old Testament the story of Gideon is the particular illustration of this principle. Israel had been in cruel bondage to the Midianites. They had been disciplined by God because of their dereliction. The discipline having served its end God had ordained their way of escape. He raised up Gideon. He called for an army and there reported 32,000 men. Then there came from God that strange word that he had too many. Too many? Can God not use 32,000? That depends upon their quality. Gideon was ordered to proclaim to the army of 32,000 that if any men were fearful they could go back home. Then there took place one of the most remarkable military movements in history. Right about face, quick march, 22,000 going home. I am not afraid to apply that to the hour in which we live. I say to you Christian men and women: If you are fearful, if you are afraid, if you think perhaps that after all Jesus is going to be hounded out of the world and defeated in the enterprises of God and go down in defeat, for God's sake clear out of the ranks. God can do more with 10,000 in whose hearts there is no trembling than with 32,000, 22,000 of whom are filled with panic.

But we are not through with our Old Testament story. Again the voice of God, I think, must have surprised the soul of Gideon. The people are yet too many. What now shall we do? These men are at war. The method of Midian's fighting is the method of ambush. You need to know where Midian is or she will track you down. Bring these men to the water. They must have water. It is necessary to watch how they take it. He brought them to the water, and 9,700 fell to the ground in their eagerness for the necessary water, forgetting that they were soldiers, and went down on all fours and drank their fill. Three hundred only bent down, stooped for their water, still alert for the enemy. And God said, With the 300 that lapped I will save you. Send back home, said God, all men who take unnecessary time for necessary things. How many of you will go home these days? How many of us will go home?

So the deep, profound question for us, who name the name of Christ, who love Him in a certain way, who love to consider His words and to watch His works, to sing His hymns, is: How much am I worth to Him for His building and for His battle? I have sung, and sung honestly, and so have you —

> Thou, O Christ, art all I want,
> More than all in Thee I find.

That is what He is to me. What am I worth to Him? Supposing He fails, how much will you lose? If He is beaten, how much have you invested in His enterprise? That is the question of all questions. Which of you going to build would not count your cost? What king, going to war, does not consult concerning the quality of his soldiers.

So let us look at these terms for a moment. The first, I will read again:

"If any man come after me, and hate not his father, and mother, and wife, and children, and brethren, and sisters, yea, and his own life also, he cannot be my disciple."

We are shrinking, we are saying that this is a terribly severe test. It certainly is. And yet is it? Is it not almost too late in the day to call that severe.

I cannot stand in this pulpit without the most poignant and shattering memories of my life crowding back upon me. I remember that August day in 1914, myself personally a broken man, I had escaped to the sea for rest at Mundesley, and there came the crack of doom. I came back, and my Staff gathered back round me. I had got some rooms here, and I went up there the first night and tried to sleep. I could not sleep. I got up and stood and I watched them going. I watched them, while they went by. Every night they went on, they went on, day after day, week after week, month after month, until five million of our boys went without conscription. I can hear them yet. The tramp of the men as they went, singing "Tipperary" sometimes. Did not these boys love father and mother? How they loved them! Did not these boys love wife and the little children who waved to Daddy as he went? How they loved them! Did not these boys love their brothers and their sisters? How they loved them! Did not these boys love life, this glorious life? How they loved it, beautiful life. But, oh, my God, an hour had struck when something bigger than love of father and mother and wife or child, brother or sister called them. I can still hear the tramping of their feet through the night. Tramping! tramping! tramping! tramping! tramping! tramping! tramping! Christ only asks of His people that they shall be as loyal to Him as the boys who followed in that appalling hour of our travail and our agony.

There are some hymns which sometimes I feel it is almost a mockery to sing.

Onward, Christian soldiers,
Marching as to war.

What do we know about war? Have we got any scars of battle? Have we ever been weakened by the way in the world's agony? I am not saying you have not, beloved. I am saying, have we? When the call of Christ comes, do we trample underfoot love and all high things when they conflict with loyalty to Him? Are we true to Him? Are we prepared to be? These are the men and women that He wants. It is almost a vulgar thing to say of God, and still I say, God but asks of the men and women who constitute His sacramental host and bear His name that they have the same spirit that actuated the boys as they went twelve years ago.

We pass to the next statement, in which He said, "Whosoever doth not bear his own cross, and come after me, cannot be my disciple." What is it to bear the cross? I have no desire to use rough language, but a great deal of nonsense is talked about cross bearing. Or if that be rough, let me put it in another way. There is a great deal of unintelligent observation made on cross bearing. I will tell you exactly what I mean. I hear Christian men or Christian women, Christian people, talking of their physical suffering, of their mental anguish, by reason of certain difficulties and obstacles, as though they constituted the cross. These things are not the cross, these things are never the cross. We have not touched the realm of the cross, when our suffering is peculiar to ourselves. These things may be His discipline, they may be His wonderful methods of preparing us for larger life, but they are not the cross.

The cross had one meaning and one meaning only. The cross is always personal, self-emptying, in order to the serving and the saving of others. You and I know nothing of the cross so long as our suffering is personal merely. But God forbid that I should seem to be saying a hard thing. My heart is in sympathy with yours, in your sorrow; but our personal sorrows do not constitute the cross, unless our sorrow is the result of a self-emptying in order that others may be served and somebody else may be saved.

What is the cross? My dear sister, member of the Christian Church, in all the graciousness of your character, do you know anything about the cross? I am not questioning your worthiness. What are you doing? You are a member of the Ladies' Dorcas Guild or Sewing Circle. You give regularly and you stitch garments for the poor. Great work, beautiful work! But that is not the cross. But do you remember one day when in your life compassion surged and flamed and you violated the conventionalities of society, and trampled upon your own fine sensitiveness and took to your arms a soiled, smirched woman. That cost you something. That is the cross!

I think back to Ancoats, Manchester, many years ago, when the great saint, Francis Crossley, whom Alexander Maclaren called Saint Francis of the Manchester slums, said a curious thing to me as we sat talking into the night after a meeting. He said to me, "Morgan, I shall never forget when first I learned the luxury of giving. I first learned the luxury of giving when giving cost me something. It was when General William Booth was just starting his Darkest England scheme. He came down here to Manchester, to address a meeting. I was sympathetic and promised to be present on the platform, and before I went I wrote a cheque for £1,000 to put on the plate. As that prophet-evangelist portrayed the submerged tenth I crushed my cheque in my hand, I was so ashamed of it. I went home to this room where we are sitting tonight and faced it out, that I was going to give what I would not miss, and I opened my desk and took my bank book and recast everything, and before morning I had put into the post a cheque which meant that for one year, at least, and more, I had to know every day the principle of sacrifice.

The luxury of the cross! Strange paradox, but tremendous truth. My dear friend, church member, church officer, it may be minister, what do you know about the cross? Our Lord says He wants men and women who can share His sufferings, make up that which is behind-hand in His sufferings, know the fellowship of His sufferings, men and women of the cross. How much are we worth to Him?

I am not going to ask for any answer. I do not think that any answer given in a crowd would be worth listening to. I am going to make no answer. But this Sabbath evening service will not be lost if, when we get home, somewhere quietly in the inner chamber with the door shut, altogether careless of human opinion — that damnable thing that paralyses us so often — and in the presence of our Lord we find out what we are worth to Him. If the investigation shall fill us with shame, He is waiting, waiting, patiently waiting, and will take us if we surrender to Him for service which the red blood of sacrifice colors, and we shall become men and women worth while to Him, men and women that hasten the building of the city of God, and the ending of the battle of the ages.

THE MEDIATING MINISTRY OF THE HOLY SPIRIT

THE WORDING of the subject as indicated marks the limits of our present consideration. There are certain facts which we now take for granted.

The first is that of the Personality of the Spirit. We speak carelessly and unintelligently, according to the light of Scripture, when we refer to the Spirit of God by the neuter pronoun "It." We should ever refer to Him, as the New Testament always does, by the pronoun "He."

Moreover, the activity of the Spirit in all history is recognized. The Spirit was active in original creation. The inspired poet of the Hebrew people declared this in Psalm 33 when he said:

By the word of Jehovah were the heavens made,
And all the host of them by the spirit of His mouth.

Our translators render this "breath of his mouth," but the Hebrew word *ruach* is often necessarily rendered spirit, and should be so rendered here. The Spirit therefore is revealed as being active in original creation.

He is also seen as active, when brooding over the chaos. "The Spirit of God brooded upon the face of the waters."

Then through the Old Testament history we find that the Holy Spirit is spoken of as coming for specific purpose upon certain men. Sometimes it is said that He clothed Himself with a man. Sometimes it is said that a man was clothed with the Spirit.

Finally, we find that the Holy Spirit prepared a Body for the Son of God in the womb of a Virgin. "The Holy Spirit shall come upon thee, and the power of the Most High shall overshadow thee." The selfsame Spirit anointed Him specifically for a Messianic ministry: "The Spirit of God...coming upon him." Our Lord claimed that He did His mighty works by the Spirit, "I, by the Spirit of God, cast out demons." And ultimately, the Spirit was operating at Calvary, for we are distinctly told that He was the Mediator of the offering of Christ, "Christ through the eternal Spirit, offered himself without blemish unto God."

All these things we take for granted, and our present study is concerned with the ministry of the Spirit in connection with historic Christianity. Here again I propose to limit myself to the consideraton of statements made by our Lord Himself concerning the ministry of the Spirit; and once again narrowing the field of enquiry, for purposes of condensation, I shall refer only to statements which He made in those final intimate conversations that He had with His own before He left them, which we now commonly and beautifully describe as the Paschal discourses.

First then we will read the statements; then survey them, then examine them; and finally make some deductions from them.

The passages to be read are all found in the Gospel according to John;

"I will pray the Father, and he shall give you another Comforter, that he may be with you for ever, even the Spirit of truth; whom the world cannot receive; for it beholdeth him not, neither knoweth him; ye know him; for he abideth with you, and shall be in you" (14:16-17).

"But the Comforter, even the Holy Spirit, whom the Father will send in my name, he shall teach you all things, and bring to your remembrance all that I said unto you" (14:26).

"But when the Comforter is come, whom I will send unto you from the Father, even the Spirit of truth, which proceedeth from the Father, he shall bear witness of me" (15:26).

"Nevertheless I tell you the truth; It is expedient for you that I go away; for if I go not away, the Comforter will not come unto you; but if I go, I will send him unto you. And he, when he is come, will convict the world in respect of sin, and of righteousness, and of judgment: of sin, because they believe not on me; of righteousness, because I go to the Father, and ye behold me no more; of judgment, because the prince of this world hath been judged. I have yet many things to say unto you, but ye cannot bear them now. Howbeit when he, the Spirit of truth, is come, he shall guide you into all the truth; for he shall not speak from himself; but what things soever he shall hear, these shall he speak; and he shall declare unto you the things that are to come. He shall glorify me; for he shall take of mine, and shall declare it unto you" (16:7-14).

We will first survey, that is glance over, them, noticing generally our Lord's description of the Person of the Spirit; what He said concerning the coming of the Spirit; and what He said concerning the work of the Spirit.

In the first statement He described the Spirit as "another Comforter," "the Spirit of Truth." Concerning His coming, He said, "I will ask . . . the Father will give." Concerning His work He said, "He shall be with you for ever." "The world cannot receive, for it beholdeth him not." "He abideth with you, and shall be in you."

In the second statement He described the Spirit as "the Comforter," "the Holy Spirit." Concerning His coming He said, "The Father will send in my name." Concerning His work He said, "He shall teach you all things." "He shall bring to your remembrance the things that I have said unto you."

In the third statement He described the Spirit as "the Comforter," "the Spirit of truth." Concerning His coming He said, "I will send him unto you from the Father," and that He "proceedeth from the Father." Concerning His work He said, "He shall bear witness of me."

In the last statement He described the Spirit as "the Comforter." Concerning His coming He said, "I will send him." Concerning His work He said, first, that it would have to do with the world — "He shall convict the world" in three respects, "sin," "righteousness," "judgment"; and in one application, that of the relation of the three matters, to Christ, "of sin, because they believe not on me; of righteousness, because I go unto the Father; of judgment, because the prince of this world hath been judged"; and secondly, concerning the church, "He shall guide you into all the truth," and, "He shall declare unto you the things that are to come"; "He shall glorify me."

To summarize. How does He name the Spirit? "The Comforter, the Spirit of truth"; "the Comforter, the Spirit, the Holy"; "the Comforter, the Spirit of truth"; "the Comforter."

What does He say about His coming? "I will pray the Father and he shall give"; "The Father will send in my name"; "I will send unto you from the Father"; "I will send."

What does He say concerning His ministry? As to the church; "That he may be with you for ever"; He abideth with you, and shall be in you"; "He shall teach you all things, and bring to your remembrance all things I said unto you"; "He shall bear witness of me"; "He shall guide you into all the truth"; "He shall declare unto you the things that are to come"; "He shall glorify me." As to the world, "He will convict the world in respect of sin, and of righteousness, and of judgment."

Now let us examine, considering first the Person as our Lord described Him. He used three definitions of the Person. He spoke of the Spirit as "the Comforter" four times. He spoke of the Spirit as "the Spirit of truth" twice. He spoke of the Spirit as the "Holy Spirit" once. The exact form of this last in the Greek is "the Spirit, the Holy." The definite article is in front of the word Spirit, and is repeated before "Holy." This gives a special emphasis to the description.

"The Comforter." John is the only one who records our

Lord's use of this word. He employs the same word again in one of his own letters. Our translators, for some reason, have rendered the Greek word "Comforter," when rendering our Lord's employment of the word; and they have rendered the same word in John's letter as "Advocate." Our Lord employed it of the Holy Spirit. John used it in his letter of our Lord; "If we sin, we have an Advocate with the Father."

Now what is the significance of the word? The word is a translation of the Greek word *Parakletos,* which in itself is a colorless word. Some words are pictorial; some words are colorless. The pictorial word is in itself a revealing picture. The colorless word always depends upon the context. It is prismatic, and gathers color from what lies round about it. *Parakletos,* simply translated, means, "called to the side of." It refers to one who is called to the side of another. That is entirely colorless until we know who it is that is called, and to whom he is called, and for what he is called. So when our Lord said, "I will send you another Comforter, another *Parakletos,*" we must gather the values of the name from its surrounding teaching.

Our translators have rendered, as we have said, by two words; here in the Gospel by the word "Comforter," and in the letter, where the word is used of our Lord, by the word "Advocate." These translations are interpretations, they are deductions; they are attempts to reveal the real value of the word as the result of declarations concerning the office of the One referred to, and they are perfectly justified. The only difficulty is that when I read one, and interpret by my English understanding, I need the other as well, to complete the significance. We want the ideas of both, when we would understand the significance of this great word.

When we speak of a Comforter today, of what do we think? Of someone who comes with comfort? Then what do we mean by comfort? Someone who comes to ease the burden or pain, or solace the sorrow? If so, our interpretation is inadequate, except as it indicates a result of that which the word really means. The word comfort came to us from the Latin *Confortare,* which is an intensive form of the verb to make strong. When the King James' translators rendered *Parakletos* "Comforter," they did not mean somebody who would sing a lullaby, but someone who would make strong.

I am not saying there is no suggestion of comfort in our modern sense of the word. There is. Our Lord said, "I will not leave you desolate," and again the Greek word is *orphans*: "I will not leave you orphans." I will come to you in the coming of the Paraclete. He comes to disannul orphanage. Yes, but the thought is not that of disannulling of orphanage by the singing of a lullaby. It is the thought of strength given, which enables us to be independent of the lullaby. Called to the side for strength, and out of the strength the sense of peace and quiet and comfort.

Advocate. That is a legal term used by the translators; and *Parakletos* was used in the Greek language in that sense. It would not be wrong to read in the letter of John, "We have an Attorney with the Father." That is exactly what the word sometimes means. A friend of mine, objecting to the word Advocate, said, "I have a lawyer, but I never call him my comforter!" But was he right? I also have had at times a lawyer, and have found him indeed my comforter, because he is at my side to undertake my case for me; all his knowledge being placed at my disposal. Thus the two ideas are not contradictory. Advocacy, the pleading of a cause, gives comfort, and the strengthening of the life.

These two ideas are dominant in the use of the word *Parakletos* as applied to the Holy Spirit. He comes to plead in me the cause of my Lord. As my Lord is my Advocate in heaven with God, the Holy Spirit is God's Advocate and Christ's Advocate in me. The offices are the same. The courts in which the work is done are different. In heaven's high court Christ is my Advocate. In this poor heart of mine the Holy Spirit is His Advocate; and in His advocacy of my Lord, He brings to me all that I need of strength; and in that sense of strength there is a sense of quietness, there is a sense of peace, there is a sense of comfort.

Again. He twice described Him as the "Spirit of truth." What is the meaning of the word truth? *Aletheia* is the negative of the hidden. That which is hidden the Spirit brings into the light. His ministry is a ministry of interpretation, and it is a ministry which reveals reality. He is the Spirit of truth, the Spirit of reality, interpreting to men. The Spirit therefore comes not only to disannul my orphanage, but to dissipate my darkness. Our Lord said, "I am the Light of the world." The Spirit comes to lead me into the light, and He interprets to me the Christ who is the Light. Our Lord also said, "I am the truth." He is the Spirit of truth, the Spirit of interpretation, the Spirit who interprets to men the thing that is true.

And so we come to the other description; "The Spirit, the Holy." That is the ordinary word for holy, but it is by no means ordinary in its significance. The word, *hagios,* literally means: awful, that which fills you with awe; but is always used to mark separation from all moral evil. It is the word that marks absolute purity.

Thus the definition once used, "the Holy," reveals the character of the Spirit; the second twice used, "of truth," describes His office, the interpretation of reality; while the one used four times, "the Comforter," describes the exercise of that office with regard to those whom Jesus was leaving behind Him and the whole world.

Let us now consider what our Lord said as to the relation to be established between the Holy Spirit and those to whom He would come. This is discovered in two brief sentences: "That he may be *with* you for ever"; "He abideth *with* you, and shall be *in* you." The prepositions are revealing; "with," "with," "in." Thus in our translations, "with" is used twice over, and "in" once; but there are three prepositions in the Greek. The first is *meta;* the second is *para;* the third is *en.* Each has a special significance in revealing the new relationship that was to be established between those to whom our Lord was talking and the Holy Spirit. "He shall be with you," *meta,* that is, in the midst of you. "He shall be with you," *para,* that is, by the side of you. "He shall be in you," *en,* that is, within you.

The threefold significance is perfectly clear. The first preposition marks the fact of His coming to be "in the midst" of them, creating fellowship among them. The second marks His coming to be "by the side of" them, for defense and comradeship. The last marks His coming to be "in" them, for power. This is technical and mechanical, but it is vital. Here our Lord, under the shadow of His cross, instructing that group of men in those last hours concerning the new age, told them that One, whom He named "the Comforter," "the Spirit of truth," "the Spirit, the Holy," would come in a way in which He had never before come. He was indicating a new permanent relationship to be established between the Spirit of God and humanity, upon certain conditions, and in doing so, He told them, "He shall be in the midst of you for ever ... He shall be by the side of you ... He shall be in you." This *Parakletos,* the Spirit of interpretation, unveiling reality; the Holy Spirit, cleansing, communicating Divine purity; shall be in the midst of you, by your side, in you.

Finally, consider what our Lord teaches concerning the ministry of the Spirit when the new relationship is established. What is to be His office, when He comes to be in the midst of us, by our side, in us? In this connection it is important to emphasize one great negative word. "He shall not speak for himself." During the last seventy-five years this whole subject of the Holy Spirit has been rediscovered after a period in the history of the church during which it was almost completely lost. It was in 1856 that William Arthur wrote his book, *The Tongue of Fire;* and since that time more books have been written on the Holy Spirit than in all the Christian centuries before that time. Every rediscovery of some lost phase of truth in the Christian church has brought a corresponding peril. One peril of this re-discovery of truth concerning the Holy Spirit has been that of declaring the necessity for the consciousness of the Holy Spirit in the life of the believer. Many so-called Pentecostal move-ments of today are making that mistake. All that is being said about the necessity for tarrying until we feel the coming of the Holy Spirit is quite unscriptural and unwarranted. When He comes, He does not come to make us conscious of Himself.

What, then, does He do? "He shall teach you all things"; "He shall bring to your remembrance the things I have said unto you"; "He shall bear witness of me." That is the ministry of the Holy Spirit, as a process. Again, "He shall guide you into all the truth"; "He shall declare unto you the things that are to come"; "He shall glorify me." That is the ministry of the Holy Spirit as to issue.

Out of all those sentences take two which summarize. The ministry of the Spirit in the church; "He shall bear witness of me," that the process; "He shall glorify me," that the issue.

Thus the ministry of the Holy Spirit in the midst, by the side, in, is one ministry. It is the interpretation of the Christ, who is the Truth. That is a process and a progress. The teaching of the Spirit is wholly concerned with the Christ.

And so also in the world. "He shall convict the world." It is important here to observe that He did not say, He shall convict the world of sin. The world does not need the Holy Spirit to convict of sin. It knows the fact of sin. This applies equally to the fact of righteousness, and the fact of judgment. He shall convict the world in respect of, that is about, sin, about righteous-ness, about judgment. He shall come to the world with a new message on these matters of which the world is already con-scious. "He shall convict the world of sin because they believe not on me." Sin has now a new center. He is able to deliver from sin, and if men will not have Him, then that is sin, the sin of rejecting Him. He shall convict the world of righteousness. Righteousness is no longer a dream, it is a dynamic in Him. He shall convict the world of judgment. The prince of this world hath been judged. The Spirit's ministry to the world is Christocentric, as it is to the church. He does not come to the world to convict it of sin, but to show the new center of sin; nor of righteousness, but to show the new possibility of righteousness; nor of judgment, but to reveal the final finding of eternity as to judgment. His ministry is wholly concerning Christ.

So in these words of our Lord, we have His declaration concerning, and His description of, the new order to be set up in the world by the coming of the Holy Spirit. This is the categorical imperative of the experience and energy of Christianity.

The genesis of Christianity as an experience is that of being born again of the Spirit.

The life of Christianity is a life taught by the Spirit and energized by the Spirit. He reveals the things about the Lord, and when men obey the light as it comes, He energizes them for that obedience, and transforms them into the likeness of the Lord.

The Spirit is also the One through whom our service is possible and dynamic. That service must be directed by the Spirit, and empowered by the Spirit, or it is futile.

Thus again, Christianity is seen as supernatural. The energy of the flesh, and the wisdom of the mind are of no avail either for life or for service. It is "not by might, nor by power, but by my Spirit, said Jehovah." This was a word spoken in the olden time. We are living in the day of complete revelation, and infinitely more, the day of possible complete realization. Whether we apply these things individually, or to our church life, or to our ministry in the world, the facts abide the same. I cannot live the Christian life by making up my mind I am going to live that life. I cannot live the Christian life by any fleshly activity or mental cleverness. I must have, and be filled with, this Holy Spirit. Our churches can do nothing which is really effective for the Kingdom of God without the Spirit. We may make a fair show in the flesh in our church life. We may have remarkable intellectual corruscations in the pulpit; but apart from the Holy Spirit there can be no preaching, and no service by the church that will reach the world. There can be no reaching of the world, save as we go as witnesses, ever remembering that our witness must be reinforced by the witness of the Holy Spirit. That was a great and daring word of Peter when, arraigned before the Sanhedrin, he said, "We are witnesses of these things; and so is the Holy Spirit." Unless there be that co-operation, all our service is fruitless service. We must be born of the Spirit. We must be filled with the Spirit; or else life and service alike must fail.

This power is available to us. Do not let us say we are waiting for the Spirit. That is not true. It may be the Spirit is waiting for us, waiting for a fuller surrender, waiting for the complete abandonment of our life to Him. Do not let us say, we wish we had more of the Spirit. That is inaccurate. It may be correct to say the Spirit wants more of us. When we are completely surrendered, He completely fills, and for life and service we are equipped in our fellowship with Christ, by the interpretation and energizing of the Holy Spirit.

THE FINALITY OF THE SPEECH OF GOD THROUGH THE SON

God, having of old time spoken unto the fathers in the prophets by divers portions and in divers manners, hath at the end of these days spoken unto us in His Son — Hebrews 1:1, 2a

THE SON — GOD'S FINAL WORD TO MAN

THE LETTER to the Hebrews has a special value today because there is abroad a very widespread conception of Christ which is lower than that of the New Testament. To illustrate what I mean by this, a recent writer has said:

> One of the best things we can say about human nature is this, that whenever a situation occurs which can only be solved by an individual "laying down his life for his friends," some heroic person is certain to come forth, sooner or later, and offer himself as the victim — a Curtius to leap into the gulf, a Socrates to drink the hemlock, a Christ to get himself crucified on Calvary.

I am not proposing to discuss that at any length, but at once say that to place Christ in that connection is to me little short of blasphemy. We may properly speak of "a Curtius," "a Socrates," but when we speak of "a Christ," our reference to Him is not only out of harmony with the New Testament presentation, but implicitly a contradiction of what it declares concerning the uniqueness of His Person.

When we turn to the letter to the Hebrews we have a presentation specially showing the separation of Christ from all others, and the reason of this is His Being and His work. Twice over in the course of the letter the writer calls upon his readers to "Consider him." In the earlier occasion he says,

> Consider the Apostle and High Priest of our confession.

and later on he says,

> Consider him that hath endured such gainsaying of sinners.

What is proposed here is that we accept that challenge.

While it is self-evident that this letter or treatise was written to and for Hebrews, its teaching is for all Christians. The writer evidently was supremely conscious of the fact that the Hebrew people were created and chosen of God to be His instrument for reaching all nations; and while dealing with the great truth particularly from the standpoint of the Hebrew outlook, he was doing so in the interest of all those who were in the purpose of God. Therefore, while the letter is a Hebrew document, it is pre-eminently a human document; and so, while Christ is presented to us against the background of the Hebrew economy, He stands in the foreground clearly revealed as related to the purpose of God for humanity.

In the opening sentences of the book we are brought face to face with a philosophy, and a definite declaration. The philosophy is discovered in the assumptions of the writer which are clearly implicated, though not formally stated. The message is found in the declaration he makes on the basis of these assumptions.

The assumptions are two; first, God; and secondly, the fact that God speaks. The first assumption, that of the fact of God, is the assumption of the Biblical literature throughout. We cannot read the first sentence in Hebrews without being inevitably reminded of the first phrase in Genesis, "In the beginning God."

Then and here, and indeed everywhere else, the fact of God is recognized, referred to, without any argument.

The second assumption is that this God makes Himself known to man, in other words, that He speaks. This at once necessarily presents God as more than an Energy diffused, or an Idea formulated; rather as having intelligence, and making known His thought to men. Later in the letter itself the writer says,

> He that cometh to God must believe that he is, and that he is a rewarder of them that seek after him.

That statement follows the assumption we have been referring to, namely the existence of God, and the fact that He does approach men, and make Himself known.

As to the declarations, they are that God has spoken to men in history in two ways. We remind ourselves again that the letter was addressed to Hebrews, and, of course, to Hebrew Christians. Necessarily its outlook is limited by that fact. We may halt for a moment and take a wider outlook. There is no doubt that God spoke to other people than the Hebrews, and in other forms, which will account for certain elements of truth to be discovered in every form of religious thought. Nevertheless we believe that His supreme and central speech to all peoples came through the Hebrew people. From that standpoint, therefore, the writer, looking over human history, says,

> God, having of old time spoken unto the fathers,

thus referring to the whole of the past economy; and continuing says,

> Hath at the end of these days spoken unto us in a Son.

If we survey the Old Testament literature, which gives us an account of what the writer refers to by the phrase, "of old time," we find that in His dealings with men, He is recorded as having spoken first through angels. No prophet or priest is found in Genesis. Then He spoke through leaders, Moses and Joshua.

He never spoke to men directly as to His government through kings. Then came the prophets. We shall find all these referred to in the course of this letter. The argument of the writer passes in review these methods of the past — angels, leaders, priests, and prophets.

We may survey the letter by imagining a Hebrew Christian reading it, and finding an answer to the things he might be inclined to say if or when, perchance, he was tempted to think that in passing from the splendid ritual of the Mosaic economy to the simplicity found in Christ, something vital was lost. He might say, for instance, The things of our religion were ministered by angels. Says the writer in reply, That is true, but the Son is greater than the angels. But, says the Hebrew Christian again, We had a great leader from God, Moses. That, says the writer, is equally true, but he was a servant in the house, and the Son is greater than the servant; and moreover, Moses, while leading the people out, was unable to lead them in to possession. That being granted, says the Hebrew, Joshua led us into the land. He did, says the writer, but he could give you no rest. The Son not only leads out, but leads in, and gives rest. Continuing, the Hebrew might refer to the great priesthood and ritualistic system of the past. This, the writer replies in effect, is all true, and was divinely arranged, but it made nothing perfect, and the coming of the Son was the coming of the Priest with the better covenant, and the better worship. And yet once more, the Hebrew might say, We had prophets who spoke to us the Word of God. That is true is the argument of the letter writer, but all they said was partial. The Word of God through the Son is full and final. Thus it is seen that the opening declaration that God spoke in times past in divers portions and manners is recognized throughout as being true. God certainly was making Himself and His way known to men through all the period. But at last, after the days of diversity and processional method, during which so much had been said, but the final word had not been uttered, He spoke in His Son.

The question arises in the mind as to the reason why God adopted this method of dealing with men. We may find help in words on another occasion, which our Lord Himself uttered to His disciples at the end of His ministry, namely,

> I have yet many things to say unto you, but ye cannot bear them now.

From these words we see that the Divine method is always characterized by a process and a progression. God had in the past many things to say to men, but He only said them as man was able to bear them. This continued until the time when God spoke to men in His Son; and the difference between the past and this, is the difference between the processional and the final. The finality of the speech of God to men through His Son is thus suggested in the opening sentences, and argued for through the whole of the writing. Here it should be said that while the speech of the Son was final, man has not finally apprehended that speech. Still the method is as man is able to bear; but now the process under the guidance of the Spirit of truth is that of the interpretation of the final speech of God.

Now we turn to consider the One referred to as "the Son." In the opening paragraph we have a sevenfold description of "the Son." He is first "Heir of all things"; secondly, "through whom he fashioned the ages"; thirdly, in Himself He is "the Effulgence" of the Divine glory; fourthly, He is "the very Image of his substance," that is of the essence of Deity; fifthly, He is spoken of as "upholding all things by the word of his power," a reference to the maintenance of the moral order; sixthly, He is revealed in redeeming activity, making "purification of sins"; finally, His administrative position is declared, "He sat down at the right hand of the Majesty on High." That sevenfold description is completed by another statement, perfecting the octave of the revelation. We are told that presently He will come again into the economy, and that when He does so, all the angels shall worship Him.

To accept this interpretation of the Son is never to be able to say, here "a Curtius," and there "a Socrates," and here "a Christ." This presentation of Him puts Him out of comparison with all others.

This Son is first declared to be appointed by God. "Heir of all things"; and in that connection the statement is made that through Him the ages have been fashioned, a declaration revealing Him as over-ruling all the movements in human history. Passing from these declarations concerning His position, the writer speaks of the essential fact of His Being, and declares that He is "the Effulgence" of the Divine glory, that is, the One through whom there was an out-flowing of that glory into manifestation. That being so, continuing, He is described as "the very Image of his substance." The margin of the Revised Version suggests that we should substitute for the word "image" the word "impress." The idea plainly is that the underlying mystery of Deity which cannot be grasped or finally interpreted by human intellect, was seen in the Son. Returning from this sublime reference to His Being, the writer next says of Him, "upholding all things by the word of His power." This reference, of course, may refer to the material order of the universe, as Paul says all things consist or hold together in Him; but I tend to the belief that the reference is rather to the word of moral authority. Once more, in what is but a passing reference, the redeeming mystery of the cross is recognized in the words, "when He had made purification of sins"; until finally it is declared that having done that, "He sat down at the right hand of the Majesty on High."

This is the Christ; this is the Son; this is the One through whom God has now spoken. Having thus described Him, the writer looking on says: "When he again bringeth in the first-born into the world." Here is one of the sentences where the translators have rendered a Greek word by the word "world," and the revisers suggest in the margin that instead of "world" we should read "the inhabited earth." I submit that it would be far better to transliterate the Greek word, and allow the sentence to read, "When he again bringeth in the firstborn into the economy." That word "economy" was in common use in the time of our Lord, and of the writers of the New Testament as referring to the Roman empire. Now, says this writer, the Son is coming again into the economy which He established, and when He comes, all angels will worship Him. This is the Son through whom God has spoken, and is still speaking.

Let me conclude by reemphasising things said at its commencement. When God spoke to men in Christ He said everything He had to say, which means that He said everything man needs to hear for his earthly life. I am careful to put it in that way, because there are things not said in Christ during the present life. Paul said in writing to the Corinthians, "Now we know in part," and the one thing certain is that in Christ we may know all we need to know for today. To that statement I should like to add that even in the ages to come, we shall still find as I believe, all our knowledge centered in Him, as it increases.

To return, however, to that limited idea, we enquire, What are the things man needs to know? That is, What are the things essential for the well-being of human nature? I should answer that the first is authority. There is nothing the world needs today more than authority; but it must be an authority that carries the consent of the governed. Human methods have constantly been those of coercing men to do things without their own consent. This always ultimately breaks down. When God spoke in the Son He gave men the one King, who, being known in Himself, whose words being rightly apprehended, man will find the authority to which he can yield himself with perfect agreement.

This very finality of authority brings with it a sense of failure, and out of this arises the next element of human need. It is that of a Mediator or Arbiter, who shall come between God and man, and act so as to bring about a reconciliation. This is perfectly provided in the Son.

Once more, having found the King whose standards condemn us, and the Priest whose redemption reconciles us, we now need a Prophet who can lead us progressively and unfailingly along all the ways of life. That Prophet is found in the Son.

A MAN WHOSE NAME WAS JOB

INTRODUCTORY

There was a man in the land of Uz, whose name was Job;
and that man was perfect and upright, and one that feared God,
and eschewed evil. — Job 1:1

IN MAGNIFICENCE of argument and beauty of style, the book of
Job is one of the greatest in literature. It is surrounded by clouds
of mystery as to authorship, as to the characters presented, and
as to the period of its writing. Moreover, there have been almost
endless discussions as to the ultimate purpose and value of it.
In earlier days of dealing with the book, I described it as "The
problem of pain." I think that may abide, but if it presents the
problem of pain, it does not afford any solution of the problem.
It is very difficult, and perhaps impossible, to crystallize into
anything like a brief statement the purpose of the book.

Nevertheless its value is that it is the Book of Job. That is to
say, it is the story of a man. Everything gathers around that
central fact; and as we read, we see this man related to the
spirit world, accessible to the approach of spiritual forces outside
his own personality both for good and evil. In other words, God
and Satan are revealed as interested in this man. We see him
also related to other human beings, his wife, and a little group
of friends gathered round him. Many acquaintances are referred
to, but they disappear, very quickly disappear, as acquaintances
do in circumstances such as those in which Job found himself.

But supremely we see him within the consciousness of his own personality. One great element of the book is that all things seem to retire, or to be retired from him, until he is alone with himself.

It is to this last phase of the revelation that I propose to devote a series of studies, Job within his own personality. Whereas as we move through, we shall hear the voices of the philosophers talking to him, we shall pay little attention to them. Eliphaz and Bildad and Zophar, and that fine young man who appears at the end, Elihu, will all be heard; but we shall do with them very largely what we have often to do with the philosophers, let them talk, while we attend to profounder matters!

I submit then, by way of introduction to these meditations, that as we take our way through this book, ever and anon we hear this man Job say things which arise out of his own deepest elemental experience. He replied to the philosophers. Thank God he did. But ever and anon, in the midst of his speech to those who were arguing with him, there welled up from the deepest of his consciousness, some challenge, some cry, some inquiry. Those are the things to which we want to give our special attention. Each one of them is elemental, and affords a deep insight into human nature.

The general thesis of our meditation is that of the answers of Jesus to Job. If there be no New Testament, or if we take away from it its essential value in its presentation of Christ, then we still have the Book of Job; it will remain in literature, but it will be the record of an unanswered agony. There is no answer to Job till we find it in Jesus. But we find an answer to every such cry of Job in Jesus.

As an introduction to this line of consideration, it is important that we refer to what we see of the man, as to his surroundings, his relation to the spirit-world, and his relation to human beings, in order that presently we may listen to him.

First, then, let us see the man. We are told his name. We are told that he came from, or belonged to, Uz. About Uz we know practically nothing. Such a place is mentioned in Genesis. Whether it is the same or not does not matter. The name passes and the location passes. It is the man we want to see. He is at once revealed in the words, "That man was perfect and upright, ... one that feared God and eschewed evil." Two words thus describe the man; and two phrases tell us the secret of his being what he was. The man is described as "perfect and upright."

We must not read into that word "perfect" all that our English word may mean. It does not mean at all that he was a sinless being. The word "perfect," the Hebrew word, simply means complete; he was complete. I think I will put the thought of that word into a phrase with which we are quite familiar. I do not know that I like it, but it will help us. It means he was an all-round man in the best sense of that word.

But more, he was "upright." The Hebrew word means straight. He was an all-round man, and he was straight. I do not know that we could pay any man today a higher compliment than to say that of him. The statement so far has not touched upon his relationship with God. It has had to do rather with his human relationships. Job had nothing in him that his fellow men could bring as a charge against him. He was complete and straight.

But the recorder also gives the secret of this uprightness or completeness of Job. He says he was one "that feared God." That is religion. "And eschewed evil." That is morality. The two things are put into juxtaposition of statement, as they always are in fact. That is the ultimate meaning of the word of Jesus; the first law, "Thou shalt love the Lord thy God"; and the second like to it, "Thou shalt love thy neighbor as thyself. On these two commandments hangeth the whole law and the prophets." Morality is ever rooted in religion. A man who is an all-round man in the true sense of the word, and who is known to his neighbors as a straight man, a man against whom men can bring no specific charge, that man has dealings with God. He "feared God." And he turned down evil — yes, that is it exactly — eschewed. He turned down evil. A man with an upward outlook, and from the upward look he learned how to deal with all the things by which he was surrounded; he turned down evil.

The remarkable fact is that according to the record, that estimate of Job was ratified by God Himself. God said to Satan the same thing about him: "A perfect and an upright man, one that feareth God, and escheweth evil." That Divine estimate is intensified, because God said of him, "There is none like him in the earth."

So we are brought face to face with a man of integrity, a man of uprightness, a man having relationship with God, turning down evil wherever it presented itself. It is very important we should remember that.

Now for the story. We watch this man, and we do so in the realm of the physical, in the realm of the mental, and in the realm of the spiritual. This man, straight and complete, fearing God, turning down evil, is seen visited by Satan, and, as a result, swiftly came overwhelming calamities. The reason of these calamities is not to be found in the man himself. That is the mistake courtly Eliphaz, and argumentative Bildad, and blunt Zophar made. They all believed that the reason of his calamity was something in himself. The book introduces him in such a way as to make it perfectly plain that it was not so. We see Job stripped of everything upon which man naturally depends on the side of the natural. Stripped of wealth, suddenly reduced from opulence to penury. Stripped of his children, who are swept out. Stripped of his own health. The vim and the virility and the vigor of his manhood all taken from him, sapped away. Presently the stripping goes further, and he loses the partnership of love in faith. I am referring to the story of his wife. Do not let us criticize her until we have been where she was. See what it meant to him. So far, wealth gone, children gone, she had stood by; and then there came the moment when her love-lit eyes looking at her man in agony, physical agony, she said, "Renounce God, and die." Which meant, I would rather know you were dead, than see you suffer. I sympathize with her. So does every woman. Yes, but get into Job's soul. She who had stood by, the companion of his faith, for very love of him is suggesting to him that he abandon his faith. He is stripped of her partnership in faith.

And still the process runs on, and it is a long one. His friends — he loses them. They came. It is an old, old story. One has often said it, but I am going to repeat it. I like these men; I like Eliphaz and Bildad and Zophar for two or three reasons. I like them first because they came to see him when he was in the darkness, when the other crowd of acquaintances had all gone. Then I like them because when they came into his presence they sat still and shut their mouths for seven days. That is a great proof of friendship, the ability to say nothing. And yet again, when they did speak, I like them because they said everything they had to say to him, and not to other people about him. The only mistake they made was that they tried to put him into a philosophy that did not hold him. He welcomed them, he was so glad to see them that he poured out his soul in a great wail of agony which he had been nursing, and then he found that they did not understand him. He lost his friends.

That brings us to the mentality of Job, his own personal consciousness. There was rooted in him a conviction of integrity which was assailed by his friends. He was misunderstood. Perhaps there is nothings worse in human life than that our lovers should misunderstand, when we cannot explain things, try as we will. In the case of Job the result was that presently he lost the sense of the greatness of his own personality. At the beginning, in the midst of the agony, he had said, "Naked came I out of my mother's womb, and naked shall I return thither." As though he had said, I am still there, whatever happens. But he lost this, and cursed the day he was born. And yet more. In the gloom and darkness, he lost his sense of God as just. He never lost the sense of God in some ways; but he did lose his conviction that God was just. God, yes, always God; but surrounded with fog and mist and mystery. God became the tragedy in his thinking. Thus we see the man; physically stripped; mentally misunderstood; and therefore spiritually, all the way through struggling, groping after a solution of God as the One who was dealing with him.

Thus, taken as a whole, with that tragic background, this Book of Job faces a fact which is everywhere apparent in human life, and which still causes perplexity. What is it? That there is suffering, and sometimes tragic and terrible suffering in the world, which is not the result of the sin of the sufferer. In this great central book of the Biblical literature, in this drama of Job, that great fact is faced; a man suffering, not because he has done wrong. We are still facing it everywhere. In every land, in city or in the country, we are faced by people thus suffering. I see at this moment in a cottage in the country a girl lying on a bed, where she has lain for twenty-eight years, suffering through no sin of her own. Thank God many flowers are there. But there she lies suffering through twenty-eight years. That is the background of this book.

If the final light may not be clear, I suggest that it shows that a human life has wider values than that of its own existence or experience; or rather, that out of the experiences of one life, there may be wider, higher values than the individual at the time may know. I will content myself now with saying one thing only. Through this man's suffering the devil's blasphemy against humanity was denied.

In the dramatic scene at the beginning, transactions in the spiritual world are revealed. The sons of God present themselves before God, the term "sons of God" being equivalent to angelic beings, the messengers of God. Among them came Satan, angelic, but fallen: and God asks him, "Whence comest thou?" There is tragedy in his answer. "From going to and fro in the earth, and from walking up and down in it." That reveals the endless restlessness of evil. Then came the question of God. "Hast thou considered my servant Job?" "Considered" is a very strong word. It means, Hast thou been watching him? Hast thou been examining him? Hast thou been going round and round the citadel of this man's soul, trying to find some way to break in? "Hast thou considered?" Now listen to Satan. "Doth Job fear God for nought?" That is the devil's blasphemy against human nature. He runs on. "Hast thou not made a hedge about him, and about all that he hath on every side?" That was true. Said the devil, "Thou hast blessed the work of his hands." Perfectly true. "And his substance is increased in the land." And that also was true.

But listen again: "But put forth thine hand now, and touch all that he hath, and he will renounce thee to thy face." The devil's blasphemy against humanity was that man serves God for what he can get out of Him. It is an old song, but it is set to many a modern tune. They are still saying it. Much of this scintillating brilliant nonsense that is being published in the form of fiction, and in essays today, is saying the same thing. They say a preacher is continuing to preach what he does not believe, because he is afraid of losing his living! They say the old lady goes to church, because of the blankets given away at Christmas. The same thing is meant when clever people talk about the rice Christians in China.

God said in effect, "Go to! try it out; take away everything." Thus Job is a battleground between God and Satan, between heaven and hell, between the truth about human nature at its deepest and the lie the devil is telling. Job went through all the process with an honesty that is the more magnificent, because at times he was hot in protest, and cried out to God for justice, and asked Him to maintain his integrity. In the end, the hissing lie of Satan the serpent was answered.

In all this there is permanent value. There are many who do not know the ultimate meaning of the experiences through which they are passing today. They are hidden away, with some suffering, some agony, some trouble gripping their hearts; not the result of their own sin. They say, What is God doing? I cannot tell them. But this book suggests that there is a meaning, and there is a value. Job through all his agony stood up, and the literature telling the story has come down all the ages, giving the lie to the devil's lie about humanity. I think it is fair speculation, that Job, in the life beyond, will be thanking God for all he passed through, if he made that contribution to the truth of God about the lie of the devil.

Taking the book as a whole, it certainly has this value also. It proves the inadequacy of human thinking in the presence of human experience. This is true both in the case of the philosophers, and in the case of Job himself. We listen to the philosophers, Eliphaz, and Bildad, and Zophar, and that wonderful young man Elihu, who began by saying, old men are not always wise; and then did some marvellous thinking. If we study all the speeches of Eliphaz and Bildad and Zophar and Elihu, we shall not find anything to object to in what they said. Their philosophy was perfectly correct and true so far as it went. Who will quarrel with Eliphaz when he says, "Acquaint now thyself with Him and be at peace?" All they said was true. But there stood a human soul, stripped and in agony, and all they said never reached him, never accounted for him. His experience defied the thinking of the philosophers.

It defied his own thinking, too. He thought as furiously as his friends, but he got no solution until there came a day in the magnificent drama when God first broke across the speech of the philosophers, and silenced them.

Just as Elihu was in the midst of his eloquence, God said:

> Who is this that darkeneth counsel
> By words without knowledge?

I think that is what God is saying today as He is listening to some of the philosophers. Who are these that darken counsel by a multiplicity of words? They may be honest, sincere; but human experience sometimes is too big for definitions, and laughs at philosophers, in its agony.

All this is equally true of Job. He tried and could not understand, and all his speeches reveal his ignorance of the deepest meaning of his own experiences.

One other thing. Taking the book as a whole, it presents a universe in which, whatever the problems, God is seen as supreme. There is no greater book in the Bible on the ultimate sovereignty of God than this. It may not explain all His methods, but it reveals Him as present and acting. Satan, the archenemy of all, wanting to prove that God blundered when He made man, suggesting that a man only fears God because of sycophancy, because of what he can get out of Him. The devil with a lie, and eager to prove his own lie. But mark the dramatic majesty of it. He cannot touch a hair upon the back of a single camel that belongs to Job, until he has Divine permission. God is throned high over evil. It is a universe in which God reigns. There is a moral center to, and basis of, all things. That is the vision that made Browning sing what some of us so often quote, because we love it so:

> That what began best, can't end worst,
> Nor what God blessed once, prove accurst.

In a final word, concentrating attention upon Job, what does the book show? A man stripped to the nakedness of his own personality, stripped to the nakedness of his own being, divested of all the things which clothe the spirit; divested of all the things upon which a man depends as he takes his way through life; those precious things – possessions, and children, and health, and love in comradeship with faith, and the friends that gather about us, and the conviction of the greatness of our own personality, and of the justice of God – Job lost them all. We see a man in the appalling majestic loneliness of his own being. Watching him, we listen to him.

In doing so I am more than interested, I am arrested and held, by the splendid argument of the man as against the insufficiency of the philosophy of his friends. But I hear more. Every now and then great essential and elemental cries come up out of the center of that personality so stripped and lonely; cries of need, cries of inquiry, cries of challenge. Then I shut the book and find no answer to one of them. It is a great thing to have heard them. It is a great thing to have had that unveiling of human need, but there is no answer.

Then I turn to the New Testament, and I see one Jesus, who began without any wealth, who went through life largely devoid of the things that others depend upon. But before I am through with Him I find He has answered every question Job asked, and supplied every need that Job revealed.

YEA, HATH GOD SAID?

Genesis 3:1-8

That is the voice of the devil. We are living in an hour in which we are very conscious that in this world of ours, and in the midst of all its affairs, hell is let loose. I resolutely use that phrase, and say hell is let loose, for hell can have no power, save under the government of God; just as Satan could not touch Job until he had asked permission, just as it is true that when he desired to have the disciples to sift them as wheat, he obtained them by asking. It is always so. That is a tremendous truth, at which we may often be puzzled; but our confidence is in God, and in the assurance that when He allows the forces of hell to be loosed, there is a reason for it, and a meaning in it. It is so in the days in which we are living.

The existence of evil, spiritual principalities, is granted by all those who accept the Biblical revelation. Words we have doubtless often quoted recently to ourselves, occurring in Paul's letter to the Ephesians, are true. "Our wrestling is not against flesh and blood." That is to say that such conflict is not final. Behind it there is something else, "But against the principalities, against the powers, against the world rulers of this darkness, against the spiritual hosts of wickedness in the heavenly places." This fact of the existence of the principalities of evil is assumed and revealed throughout the Bible; and at the head of this empire of evil is one, named variously, named Satan. We are very conscious of his power and of his deeds. It is an interesting thing to remark

219

in hurried passing, when we open our Bible, we do not find him in the first two chapters. He does not appear. And it is equally arresting that we do not find him in the last two chapters. He is not there at the beginning or end of the Bible, though, as Browning had it, "a wide compass first be fetched."

When Paul wrote to the Corinthians, he said, "We are not ignorant of his devices." That is a suggestive word rightly understood, "devices," which might correctly be rendered his mental activities, his conceptions, his purpose, his thinking. We are not ignorant, said Paul, of these things. Sometimes we are inclined to say, if Paul was not, we are. Yet it is not so. As we are men and women of faith, and followers of the Lord Jesus Christ, and believers in the Biblical revelation, we can say we are not ignorant of his mental activity, of the conceptions that underlie that activity, and of the purpose that inspires that activity. Paul had what we have, the Biblical history, with its revelation of this personality, and the story of Jesus, with the supreme relevation of this personality through His ministry. Paul had these things. So have we, and so we can say we are not ignorant of his devices.

On a memorable occasion, which Matthew records for us, Jesus uttered something which had another application, but which I venture to suggest had a wider application than the Lord then made use of: "For by thy words thou shalt be justified, and by thy words thou shalt be condemned." That is a tremendous statement, one that would bear thinking about, and illustrating in various ways. It is true that words are the expression of the inner thinking, and consequently they form the basis of judgment of the inner thinking. That is true of God. By His words He is justified, and by His words He might be condemned. Of course, that is unthinkable; and that is why the Word became flesh. It was the revelation of God.

It is equally true of man, and it is equally true of the devil. When Paul wrote, "We are not ignorant of his devices" — and I claim we stand with Paul — how shall we find out about him?

That leads us to this very simple, almost childish conclusion, the result of our knowledge of the Bible. In the process of all this literature, of the process of the story it has to tell, the voice of the devil is heard only three times. His deeds are recorded all through the record, but his voice, that which gives expression to the deepest truth concerning his personality, is heard only three times — three references to the speech of Satan in all the Bible. One is found in Genesis 3. We find him speaking again when we get to the book of Job. We never find him chronicled as speaking again until in the wilderness he confronted the God-man in the hour of temptation. Just three occasions through the Bible in which the voice of the devil is heard, uttering words which are supreme revelations of his devices, and of another fact concerning him, to which Paul made reference in another letter, "the wiles of the devil." His devices, and his wiles, that is, his conceptions, his purposes; and his tricks, the methods he adopts. Paul did not say we are not ignorant of his wiles, because we never know what they will be; but we do know the revelation that is given to us of them.

So I am asking you to stay with the devil for a little while. We are in a world in which we are confronting him everywhere. I ask you to stay and listen to him. Take these three occasions. To summarize, he is first heard slandering God to man. That is our present subject. When we hear his speech again in Job, he is heard slandering man to God. When we hear him speak again, he is facing the God-man in the wilderness.

Confining ourselves to the first, in the story we know so well, we have the account of what he said upon this occasion, and the phrase of my text introduces the whole story of the fall of man, to use again, without any apology, the old theological formula. It is the story of how man fell. We are at the source of all the rivers of sin and sorrow and desolation and damnation that have blasted and cursed human history. We are right at the beginning, and the voice of Satan is heard.

To summarize on the whole story, what did Satan do? First, he questioned the goodness of God. Secondly, he denied the severity of God. Finally, he slandered the motive of God. Here is the voice of Satan, and we are confronted with evil, with hell, with Satan. Here we are at the very beginnings, and we listen to his voice.

He first questioned the goodness of God. Notice that is only a phrase I read, "Yea, hath God said?" See what he is doing. It is an interrogative method of directing attention to something. That is what Satan is here doing. He is trying to direct attention to the fact that God is not good, that His action is not good, that God is unkind in withholding certain things. At the very beginning we are in the presence of something false. "Yea, hath God said, Ye shall not eat of any tree?" No, God has said nothing of the kind. He had said, "Of every tree of the garden thou mayest freely eat," save one. There is the suggestion that has in it the element of untruth, and that is equally so in the reply of the woman. She also was inaccurate; accurate so far, as she said, "Of the fruit of the trees of the garden we may eat"; but inaccurate when she said, "But of the fruit of the tree which is in the midst of the garden, God hath said, Ye shall not eat of it, neither shall ye touch it, lest ye die." God had not said, "Neither shall ye touch it." They might not eat of it, but here is an overemphasis of something God had said. So a lie that is half a truth is uttered in reply, and we are in the presence of the fact that the very genesis of evil in the history of man is born of the fact that the devil suggested that God was not good, was not kind. God had said nothing of the kind. He had definitely marked the limits of human freedom by the sacramental tree in the garden.

Someone may say to me, Do you really believe the story of the tree? Yes, if I believe the story of a garden. Then they may say, Do you believe the story of a garden? With what else would you start history? A city? Every city comes out of a garden. We cannot find anything in London, nothing existing in London that has not come finally out of the earth, out of the garden. We must begin in a garden. What is the sacramental symbol then? Not a ledger! Oh, it may be to some of you! The sacramental symbol is a tree, necessarily so. I do not want to stop to argue that. But the point is this: God had set there a sacramental symbol in a tree. I would not say an apple tree. It is wonderful how people have said it was an apple tree. How do you know it was not an orange? It was a tree that bore fruits, and it is called not an apple tree, but "the tree of the knowledge of good and evil." It was a sacramental symbol, and God said, No, you must not take that. That marks your limitation. That indicates sovereignty over you; and the devil entered by saying, "Yea, hath God said" that?

That is where evil always begins, and that lies at the back of the objection to law, that law limits realization, that if we can break away from law we shall be free. So we have the idea of escape and emancipation from all law. That is what we have in the world today. Lying at the back of all devilishness against which we are gathered in solemn dedication and endeavor is the idea that the God of the Bible is not good, is not kind — I mean good in that sense — and the first element of Satan's word limits the goodness of God.

Then, when we take the rest of the story, we see that he denies the severity of God. Yes, has God said you shall die? You will not. God does not mean that. You won't die. Instead of dying you will be as God is. You will be like God. You will know good and evil. He denied the severity of God. He declared that the wages of sin is not death. Again, we are in the presence of the fact that the whole of this conception is based upon an untruth. Of course, it may be almost a grotesque question how far this great prince of the power of evil believed what he said himself. Oh, he does not believe it. He knows he is lying. He knows God had not said anything that was unjust and unkind. He knew God was severe, and that His law would brook no breaking. But he was lying, and that is what Jesus meant when He said he was "a liar from the beginning." It is perfectly true. Here we have it. The wages of sin is not death. Satan was degrading man by suggesting that death was to be treated as physical only; and the moment this fruit was taken, men would still be walking about, still thinking, still knowing. Death that is not death. What Satan strove to hide is the deeper truth of the spiritual essence of human nature, and the fact that death is not the separation of the soul from the body ultimately, but the separation of the soul from God; and in the day that man ate, he died, he lost his fellowship. That is why, when God came walking in the garden in the cool, or wind, or as I prefer to translate *ruach* in the spirit of the day, came walking for communion, man was afraid.

Of what was he afraid? He had lost touch with God. He had lost communion with God. He was harboring wrong thinking about God, and consequently he became afraid of God; he died.

Yet this is always the outcome of the first fact. If we deny the goodness of God, we will inevitably deny His severity; and to deny the severity of God is surely to deny the ultimate goodness of God. If we could be persuaded that God can tolerate evil, with all its blighting, blasting effect, we could not believe in His goodness. We can believe in His goodness only as we believe in His severity. Yet here it is. This is the beginning of the whole process of evil. Goodness is misinterpreted as to its method, and people say, Oh, God is too good to punish, too good to be severe; and that means that God is not good at all. There is the lie on which this whole movement started.

Finally, and with equal brevity, the motive of God was challenged. A suggestion was made that the action of God had at its heart and center the selfishness of God, that man was being kept out of his kingdom by the law of God. That is the point at which man rebels against the government of God, or else he denies the fact of God altogether. All the story of the centuries is just the story of the fact that man has accepted these false views of God, has listened to the voice of the devil, as it questioned the goodness of God, denied His severity, and slandered His motive.

This is the first occasion upon which we hear the voice of Satan, and today we are facing the results of his calumny, the results of his slander upon God, which humanity listened to, took to, accepted, and rebelled against the government. And the issue has been the denial of God, or else denial of the revelation of God that has been granted to man in Christ.

To me it is of value to stop thus and think. I began by saying hell is let loose. We are face to face with the forces of evil as we never were in our lives before. We saw something of it twenty-five years ago, but we have never seen anything quite like this. We ask, Whence comes this madness, this iniquity of the human race? We find it in this fact, that man has accepted the views of Satan, has yielded to them, and has brought about all the sorrow and trouble that result from such acceptation. Let us realize that; and in these days when we are massed together as an empire against these things, let us wonderingly say, in spite of all our failure, God does seem in His overruling to have made us the custodians, for the moment, of the things of truth and righteousness and order.

BIBLIOGRAPHY

Biographical

The subject of this book has not received the attention given to many in the past. As a public figure and especially as an epochal teacher of the Word of God, there yet remains the opportunity for a definitive study of his life. This should be done in the historic background of his age and his contribution to the whole church assessed. Meantime we are grateful for those who have written concerning his life and work. The following abide as excellent tributes to the Servant of the Word of God.

1930. Harries, John: *G. Campbell Morgan, The Man and His Ministry:* New York: Fleming H. Revell Company. Here is an early attempt to interpret the Bible Expositor and Preacher. Written by a friend with deep sympathy and appreciation. Limited by the fact that it takes the reader through the fortieth year of Morgan's ministry and without access to private papers and records.

1938. Murray, Harold: *Campbell Morgan, Bible Teacher.* A Sketch of the Great Expositor and Evangelist. London: Marshall, Morgan & Scott. In this book no attempt is made to write a biography. There is a happy blend of the popular journalistic style treating the salient facts of the life in a general outline. The spirit of the preacher is caught again and again.

1951. Morgan, Jill: *A Man of the Word, Life of G. Campbell Morgan.* New York: Fleming H. Revell Company. This volume stands as the only "official" life and as biography it fulfills the purpose in its own context of knowledge and appreciation. The life is now crowned by the fullest information possible and, because of the access to family papers and records, we have a singular tribute of genuine human interest. Written in the context of the family it still needs a more objective study from without to show Morgan in his reading and study.

1952. Morgan, Jill. *This Was His Faith, The Expository Letters of G. Campbell Morgan.* Westwood, N.J.: Fleming H. Revell Company. In this compilation and editing there is the sweep of a full life. Subjects covered include The Bible, The Church, Christian Life and Doctrine, Death and the Future State, The Second Coming of Christ, with some General and Personal letters. Here the orderly mind of the preacher is revealed and his answers to questions are given in frankness and in sincerity.

1957. Wagner, Don M. *The Expository Method of G. Campbell Morgan.* Westwood, N.J.: Fleming H. Revell Company. Morgan is viewed as the outstanding expositor of the first half of the twentieth century and the purpose of this book is to set forth the distinctive method of his work. A demonstration is given of the relation of method to theology and theology to homiletics. A perceptive interpretation of this one facet of the preacher's skill and power of communication.

Published Works of Morgan

The list of books and booklets issued from the pen of Morgan has spanned half a century or so. Various lists have been compiled and no one is definitive. The following should be kept in mind — that Morgan edited:

The Westminster Record for four years,

The Westminster Bible Record for eight years,

The Mundesley Conference Report for eight years,

The Westminster Pulpit for eleven years.

In these appeared for the first time his sermons and Bible lectures. Later, many of these were redeveloped and took a place in the books which were subsequently published. Smaller booklets and pamphlets appeared from time to time. Certain books are now out of print or have been reissued under revised titles and often in works of several volumes. In this list the chronological order has been followed as far as it has been established:

1897 ...	*Discipleship*
1897 ...	*The True Estimate of Life and How to Live it*
1898 ...	*The Hidden Years at Nazareth*
1898 ...	*Wherein?* Malachi's Message for Today
1898 ...	*God's Methods with Man*
1899 ...	*Life Problems*
1890 ...	*The Spirit of God*
1901 ...	*God's Perfect Will*
1901 ...	*All Things New: A Message to New Converts*
1901 ...	*The Ten Commandments*
1903 ...	*The Letters of Our Lord: A First Century Message to Twentieth Century Christians*
1903 ...	*Evangelism*
1903 ...	*The Crises of the Christ*
1905 ...	*The Christ of Today. What? Whence? Whither?*
1906 ...	*The Practice of Prayer*
1907 ...	*The Simple Things of the Christian Life*
1907 ...	*The Parables of the Kingdom.* Exposition of Matthew XIII.
1908 ...	*Christian Principles*
1908 ...	*Mountains and Valleys in the Ministry of Jesus*
1907-1908	The Analyzed Bible. Introductory Volumes:
	Vol. I. *Introduction to Genesis-Esther*
	Vol. II. *Introduction to Job-Malachi*
	Vol. III. *Introduction to Matthew-Revelation*

228

The Analyzed Bible:

1908 ... *The Gospel according to John*
1909 ... *The Book of Job*
1909 ... *The Book of Romans*
1910 ... *Isaiah*, Vols. I and II
1911 ... *The Book of Genesis*
1911 ... *The Gospel of Matthew*

1909 ... *The Missionary Manifesto*
1910 ... *The Teaching of the Lesson*. A Pocket Commentary on the International Lessons for 1910.
1910 ... *The Study and Teaching of the English Bible*
1912 ... *Sunrise! Behold He Cometh*
1913 ... *The Teaching of Christ*. A companion volume to *The Crisis of the Christ*.
1914 ... *Intercession*
1914 ... *God, Humanity and the War*
1915 ... *Living Messages of the Books of the Bible:*
         Vol. I. Old Testament — Genesis to Malachi
         Vol. II. New Testament — Matthew to Revelation
1919 ... *The Ministry of the Word*
1922 ... *The Bible in Five Years*. A Comprehensive Outline of the Entire Bible
1924 ... *The Acts of the Apostles*
1926 ... *A Series of Sermons*
1926 ... *Searchlights from the Word*. 1188 sermon suggestions.
1927 ... *The Gospel according to Mark*. An Exposition of the Gospel.
1929 ... *Christ and The Bible*. A statement of faith in the Bible as the authoritative Word of God, and in Christ of the New Testament as the Son of God.
1929 ... *The Gospel according to Matthew*. A Study of the Life of Christ — His words, His ways, His works, His life and His eternal triumph.
1930 ... *Categorical Imperatives of the Christian Faith*
1931 ... *The Gospel according to Luke*
1933 ... *The Gospel according to John*
1934 ... *Studies in the Prophecy of Jeremiah*
1934 ... *Hosea: The Heart and Holiness of God*
1935 ... *The Answers of Jesus to Job*
1935 ... *Great Chapters of the Bible*
1937 ... *Preaching*
1937 ... *The Great Physician*
19   ... *The Morning Message*. A Selection for Daily Meditation
1938 ... *The Bible: Four Hundred Years after 1538*
19   ... *Voice of Twelve Hebrew Prophets*
19   ... *Peter and the Church*
19   ... *God's Last Word to Man* (Hebrews)
1940 ... *The Voice of the Devil*
1943 ... *The Parables and Metaphors of Our Lord*

1944 ... *The Triumphs of Faith*
19 ... *The Music of Life*
1946 ... *The Corinthian Letters of Paul: An Exposition of I-II Corinthians*
1947 ... *Notes on the Psalms*
1947 ... *The Parable of the Father's Heart*
19 ... *The Bible and the Child*
19 ... *The Bible and the Cross*
19 ... *Alpha and Omega*
19 ... *An Exposition of the Whole Bible*
1968 ... *The Birth of the Church*
1906-1916 *The Westminster Pulpit* — 11 Volumes of Sermons preached at Westminster Chapel, London.
1944-1945 The best of the above reissued in 10 Volumes.

—————

Booklets and Pamphlets:
Divine Guidance and Human Advice
The Romance of the Bible
Paul — What Shall I Do, Lord? — One Thing I Do
The Purposes of the Incarnation
H.M. The King, 1910-1935
Harmony of the Testaments
Sin, Righteousness, and Judgment
The Desire of All Nations
All Things New
But One Thing
To Die Is Gain
Enoch
The Fulfilment of Life
Foundations